Release

from

Despair

The Agnes Hancock Story

Release from Despair

The Agnes Hancock Story

With
JAMES McCLELLAND

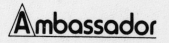

AMBASSADOR PRODUCTIONS LTD.
Providence House
16 Hillview Avenue
Belfast BT5 6JR

First Published in 1987 by Ambassador Productions Ltd.

ISBN 0 907927 19 X

Text set, printed and bound in Northern Ireland

Acknowledgements

Agnes Hancock would like to say special thanks to all those who have assisted in the production of this book and without whose help it would have been impossible.

With special thanks to Yvonne and Jim Graham, and Paul Bailie; whose friendship over the years has meant so much.

Dedication

To Pastor WALTER KELLY
for his faithfulness

To my Daughter AGNES
Her Husband NORMAN
Their Children ANNE and IRENE

To my Son GEORGE
His Wife ANN
Their Children GEORGE and JACQUELINE

To my Brother GEORGE
His Wife HAZEL
Their Son PETER

Contents

Introduction

As she stood gazing out of the living room window to the dark hills just a few miles away, a car drew up outside. It was dusk so she couldn't make out the faces of the two large, burly men who tumbled out of it. They stood back to back for a few moments as if to make sure no one was watching. Then, stepping up the drive to the front door, rang the bell.

In the few seconds it took to walk from the window to the door she wondered who this might be. Could it be the I.R.A. or some other paramilitary organisation intent on issuing further threats and causing her further heartache.

· However, she opened the door.

"Are you the faith healer?" one of them demanded, in a strong, Belfast accent.

"No," she replied, quietly.

"Well, are you the divine healer?", he persisted.

"No, I'm not," was her equally quiet answer.

The man's patience was ebbing fast.

"Well then, do you pray for people?"

"Yes," she said, "I pray for people."

"Bring him in," said the big man, beckoning towards the car still parked on the street.

"But wait a minute," she began, intending to continue with, "Hadn't you better tell me what this is all about?"

She never did finish the sentence for the big man beckoned towards the car again and called out a second time, "Bring him in".

Another large man, six foot three or more, was helped from the car and half carried up the drive and into the house.

They plonked him into the big easy chair that sat by the window and issued further instructions.

"There missus, whatever you do, do it."

It was the big man who had spoken again in that same broad, gruff Belfast accent. As he did so, he pointed to the pathetic figure collapsed in the chair opposite.

The man had suffered from a stroke and was paralysed down one side. He didn't speak, rather groaned.

She looked at him and asked, "Do you know the Lord as your Saviour?"

Once again the big man broke in.

"Listen missus, we don't want preached at. Just do whatever you do."

She approached the sick man, laid her hands on his head and prepared to pray. But before she could utter a word the big man again interrupted.

"Don't do to him different than you do to anybody else. And — don't you use oil or something? Is that the oil there?" He pointed to a small bottle which sat on the window sill.

She picked up the bottle, dipped her finger in the oil, touched the man's forehead and prayed.

When she had finished the big man spoke again, this time to his companion in the chair.

"Do you feel any different?"

The companion remained silent for a moment or two, as if doing a running check on his body, then he spoke.

"I think I feel something in this arm." He indicated the paralysed side.

12

"That's good", said the big man. "You felt nothing before. What about your leg?"

"Yes, there's some feeling in it too."

"Stand up!", the big man barked.

The man slowly stood to his feet, the first time he had done so for weeks.

Such are the stories that make up the life of Agnes Hancock.

This quiet spoken, unassuming lady has known real hardship, extreme sorrow, crippling sickness and abject poverty; yet through it all has maintained a constant faith and an abiding hope in the goodness and mercy of her God. Today, she's an inspiration to thousands as she conducts her ministry of comfort and healing to the sick.

But the most amazing story of all is that of her own miraculous healing from Parkinson's disese. That story, and the consequences of it, are the subject of this book.

1

Beginnings

Agnes Hancock was born in England but after only a couple of weeks was brought home to Ireland and spent the early part of her childhood in Bangor, Co. Down.

Their family name was McGaughey and she remembers her mother, who came from Edinburgh, as a very kind and generous woman. Her father, too, was a warm-hearted man who hailed from Bangor. She had one brother, George, and together the four of them made up a very happy family.

Her father was a pier-master and, since this work was seasonal, things were often financially difficult. So, when he got the offer of a job in Glasgow, with the promise of a house, the whole family moved there. Agnes was still very young.

One night, when she was fifteen, she was asked to deliver a message to a missionary who would be speaking at the little mission hall in Castle Street, Glasgow. Agnes was told to be there between seven o'clock and eight and to deliver the message personally to a Mr. McNabb.

She arrived at half-past seven to discover that the meeting had already commenced. Mr. McNabb wouldn't be able to see her until after the meeting, but, "Would she have a seat until then?" She did.

It was to be a meeting she would never forget. In the first place, Agnes thought the people who were there were all quite mad. They shouted things like "Hallelujah"; "Praise the Lord", "Glory", and "Amen." Some of them clapped their hands in expression of their joy. Agnes thought to herself "If I ever get out of here, I'll never be back."

Strange as it may seem, she paid little attention to the preacher, until the very end when he said, "Is there someone here who has not yet given their heart to Jesus?"

Then he asked everyone to bow their heads in prayer while a closing chorus was sung. Above the singing Agnes could hear the man's voice pleading. "If you go out of this hall without giving your life to Jesus, you could end up in Hell."

Agnes was terrified! She thought, "He's looking at me. In fact, he's pointing the finger at me."

If the door had been at the back of the hall she would have been away, but it was at the front and the only way of escape was past the pulpit — and the preacher.

Instead, she did exactly what the man in the pulpit told her to do. She went to the front of the hall to where they had a seat which he called, "The Mercy seat", and there she knelt in humble prayer.

That night Agnes McGaughey received Jesus Christ as her personal saviour — she was born again.

FIRST SERMON

Mr. McNabb had been careful to instil into Agnes the importance of being a witness for Jesus, right from the word go. However, I'm sure even he didn't expect her to be so enthusiastic so soon.

Agnes had asked him who she should tell. He had said, "How about your family?" When she asked, "What shall I tell them," he had suggested, "Just what you have heard here tonight."

So later that night, when she returned home from the meeting, Agnes preached her first sermon.

Her parents sat quietly talking on either side of the fire when she came in. Out came the finger and, just as Mr. McNabb stood pointing his, so she stood pointing hers.

"If you don't give your hearts to Jesus, you will go straight to Hell," she warned them.

At first there was complete silence. Then the storm broke! Agnes had never seen her father so angry before, and then, for the the first time, he struck her.

Her father was normally a kind and gentle man; a strict teetotaller; a man who really cared for his family and was only happy when they had everything they needed. So this sudden outburst of violence really took her by surprise.

After things had quietened down a little her mother asked, "What made you say such a terrible thing?"

Agnes told her all about the little mission hall, and the meeting, and how she had come to know the Lord Jesus as her Saviour.

Her mother didn't appreciate the testimony either. "You should have told these people that you were baptised and confirmed — and that all our names are on the church register — and that's all you need." And then she added, "You won't be going back there anymore."

But her father said, "Oh! don't stop her, she will only want it all the more. Let her go and within a week or two she will be fed up with it."

Agnes always likes to point out that that was more than fifty years ago and she's not fed up yet. Praise God," she says, "every day with Jesus is sweeter than the day before."

About three months later, at an open-air meeting, the leader asked for someone to give testimony. Agnes immediately got up on the soap-box and began to speak at the top of her voice. Little did she realise that her mother and father were standing just across the street. To them, this was the last straw.

When Agnes got home later that night she was to hear something which would alter the rest of her life.

2

Strange Surroundings

Mr. McGaughey, Agnes' father, was due a week off work and he decided to go back to Belfast, to look for work. If he was successful he would look for a house too and move his family back to Northern Ireland.

Agnes didn't like the idea of moving from Glasgow, where she was so happy, and where all her Christian friends were. So she prayed, "Lord, my dad must not get a job over in Belfast, nor a house either; for I want to stay where I am."

Even Agnes would admit that her prayer was just a tiny bit selfish. She's very glad now that the Lord had different ideas about the future of their family and that He knew better. Just two weeks later they were all on their way to a new life.

On the last Sunday before leaving for Belfast, Agnes was more than a little sad. Remember, she was still a very young Christian — just a babe in Christ really — and to be uprooted from the protective environment of the little mission hall and the people she knew and trusted, was somewhat daunting for a fifteen-year-old girl.

However, Mr. McNabb had just the right word in season for her. He said, "Jesus is in Belfast, just as he is in Glasgow, so you don't need to be afraid or worried."

He also gave her two precious thoughts to take with her. One was a promise from the Bible; "I will not fail thee nor forsake thee." (Joshua Ch. 1 v. 5) The other was the verse of a chorus:

"Leave the unknown future in the master's hands,
Whether sad or joyful, Jesus understands."

Clutching these parting gifts from the people of God in Glasgow, she set sail for Belfast and the strange unknown.

The McGaughey's new address was 86, Tavanagh Street, Donegall Road, in an area of Belfast known as "The Village".

Right away Agnes started looking for a place to meet with God's people and where she could serve the Lord.

By this time you'll have realised that she wouldn't be content in just any place. It would have to be somewhere where the people weren't afraid to shout, "Hallelujah," or "Praise the Lord." Such a place didn't seem easy to find in strange, foreign Belfast.

Her parents tried to persuade her to go out and, as they termed it, "Enjoy herself". But her only enjoyment would be found in fellowship with others of like precious faith and in service for the Lord.

Her mother had been to the local corner shop and had noticed a very nice young girl, just about Agnes' age, working there. She suggested that Agnes ought to go over to the shop and get to know this girl. Maybe they could strike up a friendship and enjoy themselves together.

So, in order to bring this plan to fruition, Agnes was despatched to Mr. Bell's shop to buy a loaf and meet this new friend. Reluctantly, but in obedience of her mother, she went.

The working of God's providence are truly marvellous and no more clearly are they demonstrated than in what happened next.

The young girl in the shop introduced herself as Jean and, with a perception rarely found in someone so young, enquired why Agnes looked so sad.

Agnes had sufficient courage to tell Jean that she was a Christian and that the reason for her sadness was that she couldn't seem to find the right place of worship.

"Oh!," said Jean, "I'm a Christian and I'm very happy at the place where I worship."

"But you see," said Agnes, "I'm looking for somewhere different. Somewhere they shout, 'Hallelujah,' and, 'Praise the Lord'."

"Then why don't you come along with me tonight," replied Jean.

It was Saturday and Agnes readily agreed to go, but just before making the final arrangements she enquired again, "Do they really shout, 'Hallelujah?'."

"Oh I can promise you that they do much more than that," Jean assured her.

"THE SALLY ANN"

When Agnes went back and told her parents that she would be going out with the girl in the shop they were delighted.

The hall that Jean took Agnes to was in Sugarfield Street, just off the Shankill Road in West Belfast.

The meeting began, as most meetings do, with hymn singing. But this was hymn singing with a difference. As soon as the opening lines of, "We're marching to Zion," were announced, two men rose from their seats, walked to the front of the hall, picked up the two flags which were there and began marching around the room. What was even more amazing was that the entire congregation also left their seats and marched around behind them.

They sang lustily; they banged the tambourines; they shouted, "Praise the Lord," and, "Hallelujah," and Agnes joined in it all, relishing every minute.

Jean had taken Agnes to the Salvation Army!

When Agnes got home that night and told her mother and father what a great time she had had, the reaction was mixed.

At first, her mother, thinking she had been to a dance or a party was thrilled that her daughter was, at last, beginning to, "enjoy herself." Her father, however, was a bit more restrained in his enthusiasm. He took the precaution of asking where she had been. When the Salvation Army was mentioned, he retorted, "Out of the frying pan into the fire!"

"But you listen to me," he continued. "There'll be no Salvation Army uniform in this house." Agnes replied, rather meekly, "Of course not."

A few weeks later, when Agnes got the offer of a second-hand uniform for ten shillings (50 pence), she couldn't resist it. The dress was a good fit, even though it was a bit stained, and the bonnet had suffered a bash or two. But when Agnes put in on she felt like the General of the Army.

However, there was the problem of her father's ban on uniform inside their house. A Mrs. Bridger solved that one quite easily by inviting Agnes to come to her house a little early and change into her uniform there.

Shortly after this Agnes was made a "Soldier", and began to fight the war alongside all the other soldiers. She attended the meetings regularly; stood in the open-air to witness of her faith and even went around the pubs in the evening selling the Salvation Army's magazine, "War Cry."

Eventually, her parents found out that their daughter was a fully fledged soldier and wearing the forbidden uniform.

However, their immediate reaction surprised even Agnes.

They were aghast that any daughter of theirs would need to wear second-hand clothes of any kind and saw to it that it would never happen again. They saved up the money and bought her a brand new uniform. And — they allowed her to wear it in the home as well.

Were they mellowing at last?

3

Full-time Service

At the age of seventeen Agnes felt that God was calling her into the Salvation Army full-time as an officer. This would require a certain amount of training and reasonable academic standards and would present her with an immense hurdle to overcome.

You see, when Agnes had been very young she had suffered from rheumatic fever and, consequently, had missed most of the early days at school. As a result she could neither read nor write. She, herself, felt that she didn't have what it took to be an officer; but God had called her and that call must be obeyed.

At first the corps captain tried to gently put her off. He didn't want her to be hurt or offended by a refusal. But Agnes persisted.

A written examination was required for entrance to the college and this was held in the officers' quarters. Agnes wondered how she would overcome this obstacle and began praying to the Lord for a way out.

What happened next, not even Agnes would dare to say was the Lord's doing.

One day, just before the examinations were due to be held, she was ironing some things for her mother. Suddenly the iron slipped and she automatically put out her hand to catch it. Catch it she did, but not by the handle; by the hot sole which gave her a serious burn.

When she arrived at the examination centre with her arm bandaged and in a sling it was obvious to the captain in charge that she could never write with her hand in that state. So, after a few hasty phone calls, it was agreed that someone else would do the writing and Agnes would just simply dictate.

In fact the person appointed to do the writing was Lieutenant Smith who, it would appear, was a very compassionate man. Agnes has a strong notion that the lieutenant believed the burn not only affected her hand, but also her mind because of some of the answers she gave. The lieutenant, in his mercy, put down the correct answers.

The written examination wasn't the only hurdle to be overcome to gain entrance to the college. There was also an interview at which, unfortunately for Agnes, the lieutenant could not be present.

After a few preliminary personal questions, which she was able to answer with no difficulty, the real test began.

"Please relate the story of, 'The Prodigal Son,' just as if you were speaking to a hall full of people," one of the examining officers requested.

Agnes could only reply that she hadn't come to that part of the Bible yet.

"Then try the changing of the water into wine," came the order.

Again Agnes had to admit that she had never read that story either.

"You don't know your Bible very well, do you?" exclaimed the officer.

"Isn't that why I'm going to Bible college," said Agnes.

"Yes, but you need some foundation to build on. You don't seem to have any at all!"

A song book was handed to Agnes and she was instructed to choose a hymn.

"Never mind the other questions, just let us hear you sing," continued the officer.

Remember that Agnes could neither read nor write, so choosing a hymn which she knew and could sing was virtually impossible. She just opened the book at random, pointed to one of the songs and said, "That one." It happened to be, "Oh happy day." Agnes was feeling anything but happy at that moment.

Next came the problem of singing it. When you can't read the words it's not easy to put a tune to them. But Agnes had a way around that too. She said, "I'm not a very good singer, perhaps you could start the hymn for me."

"Nonsense," said the examining officer, "you're far too modest." But he started the hymn just the same.

After a few bars he admitted, "At least you speak the truth." Agnes could not sing very well and the captain realised it.

What a situation she was in. She didn't know either of the two Bible stories. She couldn't sing. Yet, she wanted to be a Salvation Army officer. The examining officers thought differently and kindly advised her to go back to her corps and work hard there. Some day she would be glad she did.

When Agnes got to the door of the room she turned, looked at the three men and then said something which many would have construed to be insolent but which came right from her heart.

"Will you tell God he made a mistake when he asked me to come here? I didn't want to come but God told me to; and now you won't let me go for training. Will you please explain that to God!" With that she rushed away disappointed, disillusioned and downhearted.

However, a few weeks later, to her excited surprise, her prayers were answered. Commissioner Osborne came to their hall to hand out some special awards. Agnes nearly fainted when her name was called out and she had to go up to the platform. Everyone else who had qualified for entrance to the Bible college had been informed by letter. But Agnes was told by the Commissioner himself — and in public too!

4

Off to College

The simplicity of her faith and the child-like spirit she possessed are demonstrated in the arrangements which Agnes immediately began to make in preparation for her departure to Bible college.

A lengthy list of required items was drawn up. It included three outfits for summer and three for winter, plus all the other odds and ends needed for a stay away from home. She also had to gather up quite a sum of money to help with her keep at the college.

However, everything was left with the Lord, and before the time for her departure arrived she had all she needed, including the money.

Her mother and father sacrificed a lot and many of the people in the Sugarfield hall were very generous in their support. One in particular, Mrs. Bridger, had something for her case almost every week and Agnes Mooney and her mother also showed great kindness.

Agnes was more than a bit puzzled, however, by the instruction which came one day as she was praying — the instruction to go and buy a torch. She had no hesitation in obeying but it was a while before she realised the significance of it.

On the evening before she set sail for college there was a great farewell meeting. The hall was packed out and included in the crowd was her mother, her father and her brother. The meeting was blessed with the salvation of four precious souls and, to Agnes' delight, one of them was her mother. What joy and gladness filled her heart at that great news!

After the meeting the whole congregation marched the long way from Sugarfield Street, on the Shankill Road, to Agnes' home at Tavanagh Street. It was quite a walk but one which Agnes had been making twice every Sunday since she had joined the Salvation Army.

At the house all the neighbours came out to hear the band and the songsters, to listen to Agnes giving a final word of testimony and to bid her their fond farewells. There also came the added good news that one of the neighbours, a Mrs. Lambs, had given her heart to Jesus that night.

Next morning it was an early start to catch the boat for England. You can imagine the scene as a crowd of her friends stood along the quayside singing, "God be with you till we meet again," and the boat slipped quietly away from its moorings and sailed down Belfast lough. Agnes wiped away the tears from her eyes and a great feeling of loneliness welled up within her.

Arriving at college was a wonderful experience! Here was prayer answered, another step of faith taken, another chapter in her life opening up.

She was shown to the room that would be hers, given a list of her chores and began settling in to college life. But even in the midst of all this elation there was a turmoil going on within. She wondered how long it would take them to find out that she could neither read nor write; and what would happen when they did?

It was usual for new entrants to the college to be given some preliminary tests; the first one was for reading. When

Agnes went for this test she told the officer in charge, truthfully, that just before she had left home she had to have all her teeth removed and a new set fitted. This had left her with an extremely sore mouth. The officer sent Agnes to see the nurse who immediately excused her from all duties and classes for two weeks.

However, it didn't mean that Agnes got away with anything. When she got back to her studies she discovered that she was the only trainee in the whole place who would have to attend all the special classes.

At the very first lecture everyone was given a sheet of plain paper on which to make notes. Agnes, as you know, couldn't write, so she sat and scribbled. Again she wondered how long it would be before they would find out about her; and what would happen. Would they send her home? Her situation was the subject of much silent, fervent prayer.

What Agnes did not know was that God had already met her need. She was sitting right next to Agnes in class and her name was Cadet Orr.

Another interesting little snippet can be added here which sheds light on the way that normal things were turned to her advantage.

Christian names were not allowed to be used at the college. Everyone was addressed by their title and surname. Hence — Cadet Orr. You'll remember that Agnes' surname was McGaughey (only Scots or Ulster people will really know how to pronounce that) and since it was so difficult to get the tongue around, she was rarely called on to give answers in class.

But back to the classroom. Cadet Orr had been watching the scribbles of Agnes for a time and couldn't help asking, "Why have you been scribbling instead of taking down notes? Have you a good memory or something?"

On hearing that Agnes was illiterate she asked, "How did you get in this far?" Agnes replied, "God got me in!"

Cadet Orr's response was tinged with a touch of humour. "He'll have to work overtime to keep you here then."

Agnes and Cadet Orr struck up a close and blessed friendship which was really to be the means, under God, of Agnes making it through college.

Shortly after the classroom incident Agnes told Cadet Orr about the purchase of the torch. Now the rules in college were — up at six o'clock in the morning; light out by ten o'clock at night. Agnes said, "Now I know why God told me to buy the torch. I will be up earlier and go to bed later, that way I'll catch up with my studies."

"But," said Cadet Orr, "what good will that do you if you've no one to help you? Perhaps God wants me to do just that."

The weeks and months that followed were to be unforgettable to Agnes. Cadet Orr helped her with all the studies and also taught her to read and write. Agnes seemed to pick up everything in no time at all so that, within a few months, she was writing her first letter home.

It was no work of literary genius, but it was the first letter she had ever written. How thrilled Agnes was to pop it into the letter box and how thrilled her mother must have been to receive it.

By the mercy of God and with the help of her companion, Agnes' successfully completed the full course of training, even coming out with some excellent results. On her final examination paper she got 79% and for her final lesson work 83%. Not bad for a girl who, at the beginning of the course, could neither read nor write.

5

On the Front Line

With her training successfully completed Agnes launched
out on what the Salvation Army call, "field work."

Her first appointment was to the Toxteth area of
Liverpool under the direction of a Captain Mercer.

It's interesting to note that her first pay was 9 pence per
week while the captain got 10 pence. When Agnes asked
how they were supposed to live on that she was informed by
the captain, "Oh, we live by faith."

In the mornings Agnes stayed in to do the housework
while the captain went visiting. Just about twelve o'clock
she met the captain at a pre-arranged spot and then they
went, "on call."

Mrs. Dunne was a sweet lady with a soft spot for the girls
of the "Sally Ann." She always had the tea-pot on and
something good for them to eat. As a result of such kindness
they never ever went hungry, God, through His children,
providing all their needs.

Agnes loved this new work and threw herself into it with
heart and soul. She counted it a wonderful privilege to be
involved in furthering the work of God.

After only eight months she was asked to take charge of a
corps on her own. She spent times of service at Bootley

Ormskirk, Southport, Wallasey and at Peel, Laxey and Ramsey on the Isle of Man.

Just after war broke out she was transferred to Aintree, near Liverpool. Most of the time there was spent helping people who were suffering as a result of the blitz. Some had lost loved ones, some their homes, some everything they possessed.

The nights were spent in Lime Street underground railway station serving tea and sandwiches to all who came for shelter. The same families came every night with each mother having a little part of the station which she called her own. Some even fitted up sheets to make their area a bit more private.

When the bombs began to fall everyone huddled together and sang choruses to keep their spirits up. The louder the bombing the louder the singing and when, eventually, the "all clear" sounded there would be a prayer of thanksgiving to God for His safe keeping through another night.

During those dark days and nights the Lord worked wonderfully in the hearts of the people and many came to know Jesus Christ as Lord and Saviour.

Life in the Salvation Army was never dull and Agnes remembers many an amusing experience.

Like the time when thieves broke into their quarters and stole the money raised from the sale of the "War Cry" and "Young Soldier" magazines. The stealing of the money wasn't so funny but the sequel certainly was.

The local butcher heard about the incident and pointed out that they needed somewhere really safe to put the money — somewhere that no one would ever think of looking.

He presented them with a cardboard joint. It looked like a piece of real meat with all the colours, etc., but it was hollow inside and just the place to hide the money. The butcher also suggested that they put this in the roasting tin, pour a little melted fat over it and leave it in the oven. No thief would ever dream of looking there.

The butcher's instructions were followed to the letter and the idea worked perfectly; that is until Agnes' mother came to visit. Agnes had to go out urgently to visit someone who was sick. As she left she called out to her mother, "I'll make you something to eat when I get back again. You make yourself a cup of tea in the meantime."

But mother had a different idea. She would have the whole meal ready when her daughter returned. So she washed the potatoes, prepared the vegetables and — turned on the oven to cook the meat. By the time Agnes returned Mrs. McGaughey was wondering what the awful smell was and even suggested that Agnes had been sold "a bad piece of meat."

Agnes rushed to the oven and pulled open the door. Her precious money had certainly got a roasting. In fact there wasn't very much of it left. However, the bank was very understanding and, since the serial numbers on the notes were still identifiable, changed the whole lot for new ones. I'm sure the staff had a good chuckle about it too.

On another occasion when some friends from Belfast came to stay for a while, Agnes was very anxious to deliver a fine sermon at the meeting. She spoke on Luke Ch. 2 verse 40; the story of Christ sitting in the Temple amongst the learned men.

Agnes wanted to bring out the point that whilst it took only one day to lose Jesus, it took three to find him. She went to great pains to emphasise how Joseph and Mary, when they discovered that Jesus was missing, went through all the compartments of the train asking if anyone had seen him!

Amazingly, some of the people saw nothing funny in the fact that Agnes had the people of Bible times riding on trains long before they were invented. However, her friend

Sam Thompson had great difficulty in suppressing his laughter and was almost overcome by it. Agnes could detect that something was wrong; that she had made some kind of gaff; but, of course, it wasn't till after the meeting that she found out the true nature of her departure from fact. Thankfully, she was able to laugh at her mistakes as well as learn from them.

When stationed at Peel, on the Isle of Man, she was very keen to get some of the fishermen to the services and decided that the best way of succeeding would be to show a healthy interest in their work.

When the boats tied up at the harbour Agnes was there and at the first opportunity enquired if the catch had been good that day.

"Yes," came the reply, "we've got a lot of herring today."

In her innocence Agnes asked if they had caught any kippers.

The fishermen looked at one another for a few moments without uttering a word. At last, one of them spoke up and informed Agnes, "It's tomorrow we catch the kippers Maam. Would you like to come with us?"

Agnes would have done anything to get those men into the meeting, so next time they put to sea she was with them, dressed in oilskins, sou'wester, boots, etc.

When they were well out to sea the fishermen explained to Agnes exactly how kippers were caught.

"We don't catch kippers in nets," they said. "We have to fish for them with a line and a hook."

They duly supplied Agnes with a line, baited it, and invited her to hold onto it, wait for a kipper to bite and when it did, give it a good tug. After about half an hour the signal came to pull up the line and there on the end of it was Agnes' kipper.

Of course she realised her mistake right away and knew

that the only thing she could do was to have a good laugh about it.

Her time wasn't entirely wasted though. While those men had a good laugh at Agnes' expense, they were really laughing with her and many of them became her friends from that time on. Quite a number of them came to the meetings and those who had children sent them along too. And there was the added bonus that from that time on she always had an adequate supply of fish.

Agnes remembers her years in the Salvation Army with great affection.

There was the wonder of seeing men and women trusting Jesus Christ as Saviour. There was the thrill of watching those who were saved progress to a closer walk with God. There was the joy of ministering to those who were sick, suffering, bereaved or troubled. And there was the satisfaction of her own growth in grace too.

She watched young couples being married, dedicated their little ones to Christ, laughed with them in their times of gladness and wept with them when sorrow came. Whatever was done, was done in the name of the Lord Jesus and for His glory.

Yet, despite all this, Agnes looks back on those days with a measure of regret, for she eventually left the Salvation Army. It's an area of her life which is painful to think about and almost impossible to talk about, and, although she knows that God has forgiven her many years ago, she still feels that she failed Him in leaving His service prematurely.

However, what was to happen in the future would prove that the God she served was a God of mercy, compassion and grace.

6

Tragedy!

It is one of the most natural things in the world for young people to fall in love. Agnes was no exception and, whilst working in the Salvation Army, she met and was attracted to another young salvationist. After a time they planned to be married.

However, the rules in the Salvation Army concerning the marriage of officers are quite strict. Briefly summed up they are as follows. When a male officer marries, the woman he marries immediately assumes his rank. Equally, when a woman marries she assumes the rank of her husband, whether it be higher or lower. Since Agnes was a captain, and the man she was marrying had no rank, she would automatically lose her commission as an officer.

Agnes chose to resign her commission and, shortly after leaving the Salvation Army, was married to James Hancock.

He was a strong, muscular, healthy man, the very epitome of fitness. I suppose that's why, when war broke out and he joined up to serve his country, he found himself in a commando unit.

Army service and the demands of war put great restraints on family life in those days and James was away from home most of the time. The short times of leave were the only opportunity he had to see his young wife.

In due course her first child, a daughter, was born and she named her Agnes, after her mother.

Shortly after the war ended and, of course, her husband came home for good. He had already dedicated his life to the Saviour and planned to go back into the Salvation Army as an officer. Already, all the necessary arrangements had been made. It was also agreed that Agnes would accompany him. The future seemed to be opening up with bright and fair prospects.

But it seems that tragedy always chooses the most inappropriate moment to strike. Nowhere is that more true than in the life of Agnes.

One morning she awoke and came downstairs at the usual time, to make the breakfast. She left her husband in the bedroom, playing with their year-old daughter. When the breakfast was ready she called him but there was no reply. Going back upstairs she found him lying stretched across the bed — lifeless. The Lord, in his wisdom, had called him home. Just two weeks later Agnes gave birth to their son, George.

She here she was, a widow with two young children and very little means of support. In a moment of time her world seemed to have turned upside down.

Shortly after this she went to live with her father and mother who were still in Glasgow. Her father was the janitor at a local school and was able to give her some support. However, the cruel hand of tragedy was not to be shaken off so easily, for, in a few months her mother was also taken from them.

Agnes did not miss the opportunity to witness for her Lord and asked her father what would have happened if he had been taken in death, rather than his wife. The arrow of conviction struck home and Agnes had the joy of leading him to a knowledge of sins forgiven through faith in Jesus Christ.

The work of grace wrought in his heart was not a mite too soon, for within the space of a few short months he, too, was taken home to Heaven. Once again Agnes was left alone.

In the midst of all this sorrow and desolation one promise from the Bible became very precious to her. In Hebrews Ch. 13 verse 5; God promises, "I will never leave thee nor forsake thee." Agnes can truly testify to the truth of that promise for she leaned upon it many times during those dark days.

After the death of her father she moved to a house in the Garthamloch area of Glasgow and made an attempt to settle down again.

There was no Salvation Army hall nor other suitable place of worship in the area so, on her first Sunday morning there, since she couldn't afford to travel any distance, she had a quiet time of prayer alone with her Lord.

As she prayed the Lord spoke to her very clearly, it seemed, and told her to look outside. When she did she noticed a lot of children playing in the streets. The Lord immediately laid upon her heart a burden for these children and a plan for a Sunday-school began to form.

Other Christians, namely John Gilchrist, Mary McCafferty and a Mrs. Wilson, had a similar burden, so together they joined forces, opening their new Sunday-school in a classroom of a local day-school. The Lord blessed their efforts and precious young lives were transformed by the grace of God.

After some time a Sunday evening service began also, with a mid-week prayer meeting and Bible study being held in Agnes' home.

By this time Agnes was working full-time as a home help and, of course, she had her two little children to look after.

But, she was able to manage all this as well as finding some time to visit the sick.

As the work grew and became more widely known they were asked to travel to other areas to conduct meetings. One of the places they visited from time to time was the Elim Church in Glasgow where an Ulsterman, Walter Kelly, was the pastor. Her meeting with Pastor Kelly was to be of great significance in years to come.

Back at Garthamloch the meetings continued regularly and, on at least one occasion, with startling results.

On this particular Sunday night some visitors from Pastor Kelly's church were conducting the meeting. In the middle of the service about 20 young lads from a local gang burst into the hall and, brandishing a knife, began to threaten those who were there. Perhaps they were only intent on frightening people. If that was the case they were eminently successful!

Agnes asked them to be quiet till the end of the meeting when she would speak to them. When the time came and everybody else had been allowed to leave peacefully, Agnes went as agreed, to speak with them. Immediately the knife came out! For a few moments she tried to reason with them but they just laughed and ordered her away.

She turned to go but after only a few steps a voice seemed to say to her, "No one loves these lads. No one wants them. But I'm their Lord just as I'm yours." Agnes felt she must go back and speak to them once more.

"I was wondering, boys, if you'd like to come to my house and I'll have a meeting especially for you?" Then she gave them the address, 999, Gartlock Road.

They all laughed at the mention of 999, it being the same as the police emergency number. But Agnes pressed home the invitation with a response to their laughter. "At least you won't forget it, will you?"

They called her a "head-case" and "a nutter," but after

some more bantering and laughter they agreed that Thursday of the following week, at 7.30 p.m. woud be fine for the meeting.

Agnes asked Mrs. Wilson, a true saint of God, to help her and arranged for a man who was experienced in dealing with these young people to be the speaker.

At 7.30 on the Thursday night Agnes looked out of the window not knowing what to expect. She could hardly believe her eyes. Coming up the street from one direction was the gang of boys she had spoken to and they were accompanied by a number of girls. Coming down the street from the other direction was another gang of boys and girls.

Hasty telegrams of prayer were shot off to Heaven while the speaker and Mrs. Wilson ran to put out more chairs. When the gangs came in they were placed on either side of the room with the speaker in the middle.

Agnes made them all very welcome, asked that they come and go quietly and everything passed off peacefully that first night. In fact, for the next eighteen months, upwards of 40 young men and women attended the meetings in Agnes' home every week and there was never any trouble of any kind. Many of them found Jesus Christ as Saviour and could look back on those days as the time when their lives were changed for the good.

Sadly, however, it all came to an end. One day a particular letter arrived with Agnes. The letter came from the local housing office and stated that a notice of complaint, signed by over 100 people, had been presented to them. If the meetings didn't end within 14 days Agnes would be served with an eviction order.

Despite the fact that over 3,000 people petitioned the housing office to allow the meetings to continue, and that none of the neighbours had signed the letter of complaint, the meetings had to come to a close.

However, they did so in a blaze of glory and with a

shower of blessing. On that very last night the house was packed. The presence of the Lord filled the place as never before and when the preaching was over and the appeal made, six young people, including the two gang leaders, gave their hearts to Jesus Christ.

Altogether, over the months, some fourteen souls had been brought to Christ. Many of them are still actively engaged in the Lord's work and one of them went as far as the foreign mission field.

The meetings re-opened in a classroom of a big new school but the young people only came to it for a short time. For some reason the atmosphere wasn't the same as in the house and the meetings eventually came to a complete stop.

Perhaps it was all in the providence of God for within a very short time Agnes was to be tested in a more severe crucible than ever before. She would not be able to give a lead in the Lord's work for many a long day.

7

The Broken Body

For quite some time Agnes had noticed a serious deterioration in her health. A persistent trembling had developed in her hands and arms and she found it very difficult to continue with all the work which normally she loved doing.

The problem eventually became so serious that when she went visiting the homes of people she refused the customary cup of tea because she couldn't hold it steady. And when she was preaching the Bible had to be left down on the desk all the time for the same reason.

·She had no idea what was wrong and was afraid to go to a doctor for fear the news would be bad.

Then one Sunday morning she got up feeling very ill. By now she realised that there was something seriously wrong with her health. She began to worry and fret about the children and pleaded with God that she might be all right until the children could look after themselves.

Just then her door bell rang and when she went to answer it her good friend Mrs. Wilson stood there. Mrs. Wilson came in and announced that the Lord had told her to take Agnes to the Elim church that morning.

"You go and get yourself ready, I'll see to the children," she said.

Agnes protested that she didn't feel very well that morning but Mrs. Wilson wasn't taking any excuses.

Agnes will never forget that service. When they went in the congregation was singing the chorus:

> *"We worship and adore thee,*
> *Falling down before thee"*
> *Songs of praise ringing,*
> *Hallelujahs singing,*
> *Hallelujah, Hallelujah, Hallelujah."*

The power of God was so real that Agnes forgot all about herself and her troubles, just fixing all her thoughts upon the Lord.

When Pastor Kelly invited all those who knew the Lord to take part in the breaking of bread service, Agnes wondered if she dare.

The Salvation Army don't have a communion service so, even though Agnes had been saved a long time, she had never had the privilege of sitting at the Lord's table.

Mrs. Wilson assured her that, since she was a child of God, she was perfectly entitled to take of the bread and the wine, thus remembering her Lord's suffering and death. And she did.

It was truly a blessed experience. Jesus himself drew near and Agnes felt lifted up into the heavenlies. She longed to be able to do this every Sunday and whispered a prayer that the Lord might just make it possible.

To her surprise, a few minutes later, Mrs. Wilson leaned over and said, "The Lord has just told me to use part of my tithe to bring you and the children here every Sunday morning!" Mrs. Wilson turned out to be as good as her word and brought them to the church every week until Agnes' health made it no longer possible.

At that first service in the Elim church Pastor Kelly had also invited Agnes along to a baptismal service they were holding on the following Thursday evening. It was to take place in the Pollick Baptist church.

As Agnes watched those, who in obedience to the Word of God, were following Jesus in this new way, it was an unforgettable experience. This was something Agnes had never done either but something which she felt must be remedied right away.

She enquired of Pastor Kelly when the next baptismal service would be held and was told that, since they were depending on the use of the Baptist church, it would be quite some time.

Agnes knew that her illness was catching up with her fast and that she wouldn't be able to wait very long. Therefore, she was overjoyed to read in the paper, that very week, that the Pollick Baptist church were to have a baptismal service of their own on the following Sunday night.

After a lot of earnest pleading with the pastor and office-bearers of the Baptist church, to whom you must realise she was a total stranger, it was agreed that Agnes could be baptised at their service.

She will never forget the thrill of that wonderful experience and the joy that filled her heart as, after all these years of knowing the Saviour, she finally obeyed Him in going through the waters of baptism.

Even the promise that was given her that night seemed most appropriate.

> *"When thou passest through the waters, I will be with thee; and through the rivers, they shall not overflow thee: when thou walkest through the fire, thou shalt not be burned; neither shall the flame kindle upon thee. For I am the Lord thy God, the Holy One of Israel, thy Saviour."*
>
> Isaiah Ch. 43 v. 2–3.

Little was Agnes to know how very near those waters were and how soon she would be going through them.

As she went to work that next Monday morning she felt very close to God, perhaps closer than ever before. She felt she was at the very centre of God's will for her life and her heart was full of praise and gratitude to Him.

She had just begun her daily round of work as a home-help and was still in the first house when, suddenly, she was taken by a fit of dizziness. It seemed as if the room was spinning around her! She grabbed hold of a chair to keep herself from falling to the floor. The old lady, for whom she was working, tried to help her, but she was 89 and didn't have sufficient strength. A neighbour was sent for, who came and helped Agnes into a chair, and then sent for the doctor.

The doctor, a stranger, was very kind and drove Agnes home. On the way he talked to her about the necessity of going into hospital but she explained that she had two small chldren and that hospital, at this stage, was out of the question.

However, when he had driven her home, he immediately contacted Agnes' own G.P., a Doctor McEwan. He agreed with the first doctor's recommendation that hospital, immediately, was imperative.

Agnes remembered that the people of the Tent Hall, in Glasgow, ran a home for underprivileged children. Someone phoned the person in charge and, within an hour, she was there, assuring Agnes that the children would be well looked after until she came home from hospital.

That first spell in hospital lasted for ten weeks. Numerous tests were done for the first six weeks and then one day, quite unexpectedly, the doctor walked in and asked her who her next of kin was.

She had a brother living in Bristol but, since that was so far away, she thought there was little point in giving his name. Instead she gave the name of the Elim minister, Pastor Kelly.

Although Agnes wasn't a member of the Elim church, Pastor Kelly came right away. He seemed to know what was wrong even before Agnes did and prayed that God would meet her every need. He asked the Lord to give her His peace and comfort in the coming days.

Then the professor came in. Agnes sensed that the news would not be good.

The professor spoke kindly and softly but his manner did nothing to deaden the blow of the message he had to deliver.

"I am sorry to tell you," he began, "I am sorry to tell you that you have an incurable sickness called 'Parkinson's disease'."

His words came like a death sentence so that she hardly heard what followed.

"This sickness is travelling through your body at an alarming rate. In a very short time it will be difficult for you to look after yourself, not to speak of your children. I am of the belief that if would be best for both you and the children if you would agree to them going into care."

At that moment Agnes' arm began to pump up and down like the piston of a steam engine. She pleaded with the doctor to do something to stop it but there was nothing he could do.

"My dear, I wish I could stop it. But it's part of the illness. It's called a locomotive action and there's nothing anyone can do to stop it."

And that's how it was for the duration of her long illness. At first just the arm. Then a leg. Eventually, her whole body was affected by this crippling disease until Agnes became the mere shell of her former self. At times, even her mind seemed to be affected and tortured by this hopeless affliction.

The amazing thing is that, through it all, she never lost sight of her faith in God. God's love was always real to her and stayed with her through those dark, impossible days.

What happened next reads like something from a Charles Dickens novel but it's all absolutely true!

8

Christmas

Agnes was discharged from hospital on the morning of Christmas Eve. She was only allowed to go because it was Christmas and because the home where her children were being looked after was closing for the holiday period.

There was to have been money from the Social Security service so that the three of them could eat and to help provide some Christmas presents for the children. However, that money wasn't there.

They had no food, no coal, not a thing for the children — and no money!

A friend, Mrs. McCafferty, came to see how they were and brought a jug of soup. How glad they all were to see that. Mrs. McCafferty didn't have much herself but, on Christmas morning, she sent Agnes half of her bread so that she and her children wouldn't starve.

And then the miracle Agnes had been praying for happened!

She had been awake most of the night praying and seeking God for an answer to her problems. She wondered if this was God's way of telling her that the children should be taken into care after all.

"If not Lord," she prayed, "would you please send us

enough to get a little coal, some food and something for the children for Christmas?"

Christmas morning came and it seemed as if there wouldn't be any answer to her prayer.

Then the door bell rang and her little daughter ran to answer it. There stood the postman with two parcels each for the children and a registered letter for Agnes.

When the letter was opened out fell a wad of five pound notes — fifty pounds altogether.

"Fifty pounds!" exclaimed Agnes. She had never had so much money at one time before and was certain there must be some mistake. But a little card along with the money dispelled her doubts immediately.

It said, "Jesus knows your need. This is why He told me to send this to you."

It was unsigned but Agnes couldn't help thinking of the scripture which proclaims, *"In as much as ye have done it unto one of the least of these my brethren, ye have done it unto me."* —(Matt. Ch. 25 v. 40).

If this had been a city in England or N. Ireland things might not have turned out so happily, but, since Christmas isn't such an important holiday in Scotland as elsewhere, the story has a truly happy ending.

Just around the corner there was a shop which stayed open on Christmas morning until about lunch time. The two children were despatched to that shop, to get anything they thought would be needed for the house, plus whatever they wanted for themselves.

Remembering that, "Freely ye have received, freely give," Agnes took care to be just as generous to her neighbours as God had been to her. Mrs. McCafferty, the kind lady who had shared her soup, and some of the others who lived in the same tenement, enjoyed the good things which the Lord had provided that day.

But the miracle wasn't over yet!

While the children were at the shop the door bell rang once more. It was a great struggle for Agnes to get there but she finally managed it.

This time it was the coalman who announced, "I've come with your Christmas gift."

He left two bags of coal and a bag of sticks, and, as if that wasn't kindness enough, proceeded to light the fire.

Agnes insisted that she could pay for the coal and sticks, but the coalman wouldn't hear of it.

"Don't thank me, thank Jesus," he said, and with that he was off. This was his Christmas gift to her. And what a memorable Christmas it was.

Agnes' illness made it impossible for her to look after herself properly and so she was given a home help.

The first lady appointed to the task only lasted for a few weeks and then she asked to be replaced.

Her successor, Betty Stevenson, Agnes regards as the nearest thing to an angel on this earth. She was to be Agnes' constant friend and helper for the next seven years.

Betty's main responsibility was to look after the house, keeping it clean and tidy, etc. But she went far beyond that call of duty, helping in every way she could and becoming, to all intents and purposes, a nursemaid to Agnes.

The illness had so advanced by this stage that Agnes couldn't even do such simple things for herself as looking after her own personal hygiene. But Betty always made sure that she was clean, fresh, comfortable and fed.

Betty's husband, too, was a great help. He came and dismantled the bed, just leaving the mattress on the floor, so that Agnes could crawl into it more easily.

He also fixed the snib on the door at a lower level so that, if an emergency happened and Agnes was alone in the house, she could always get out. In fact, Agnes could open the snib with her mouth.

Young Agnes was not yet ten years old, yet as she grew

up, she was a tremendous help to her mother. When other children would be out playing in the streets she was in the house preparing meals and doing household chores, like washing and ironing, which the home help didn't have the time for.

Little George did his share too, running errands and doing whatever he could to help his sister run the home as smoothly as possible.

There was just a year between the two children and it was a great encouragement to Agnes that they both, early in life, had given their hearts to the Saviour.

As she looked at them Agnes would often pray, "Lord, spare me until they can both work and look after themselves."

In the providence of God her prayer was to be answered in a way that even she could never have imagined.

Her great concern for the children prompted her to do everything she could for them. But she was also anxious as to what might become of them if anything should happen to her.

She already had a "penny policy" on her life but thought it would be a good idea to have something extra, in the event of her death, so that the children would be better provided for.

So, one day when the insurance man called she had no hesitation in putting this suggestion to him.

The poor man didn't know what to say. Rather than offend her he put her off for the time being by saying that he would have to bring the inspector to talk to her.

The inspector was as kind as he could be but had to explain that there was just no way that any insurance company would give life cover on someone as ill as Agnes. Furthermore, the very fact that she was suffering from Parkinson's disease would prevent their paying out anyway.

What a change those men were to see in a few short weeks! A change that even Agnes would hardly have believed possible.

9

Into the Depths

Friday the 17th of September, 1959, is one day that Agnes will never forget.

It began just like any other day, with the chldren going off to school as usual. They left the snib of the door unlocked so that Betty, the home help, could let herself in.

Betty never came that morning. She had rather a bad cold and had telephoned the office to say that it might not be a good idea to go to Agnes', in case she passed on her germs. The office had arranged for someone else to go in Betty's place but, for some reason which was never discovered, that person never turned up.

By about half past ten Agnes was longing for a cup of tea and decided to have a go at making it herself.

Now remember that she was virtually a cripple, only able to crawl about the floor on her wasted legs, and with no use of her arms at all.

Using her mouth she managed to haul two chairs over to the sink and push them together. Then, somehow, she managed to climb up on to them.

Grasping the handle of the kettle in her mouth she dropped it into the sink and then, again using her mouth, turned on the water tap.

The next problem was to transfer this kettle of water onto the gas stove. But, again, this was accomplished, after a great struggle. It was a comparatively easy job to turn on the gas tap, which lit the gas automatically.

After a little time the kettle came to the boil and, immediately, presented Agnes with another serious problem. The kettle began to boil over, spurting hot water from its spout, and splashing it down over the gas tap. This meant that Agnes could neither turn off the gas nor could she move the kettle.

This entire operation, which would have taken the normal, healthy person a matter of minutes had taken Agnes hours to complete.

She was still grappling with the problem when a voice suddenly called out:

"Mum! You're not allowed to do that."

It was her little daughter Agnes who had just come in from school. The time was twenty past four!

The suddenness of the child's cry, in a house which had been quiet all day, startled Agnes. Her head, which she had difficulty in controlling at the best of times, fell forward on her shoulders, banged against the kettle and toppled it off the stove.

The boiling water spilled everywhere, including over young Agnes, who had dashed over to help her mother.

Her cries of agony immediately filled the house, alarming young George, who was just coming in and alerting the neighbours who lived in the other parts of the tenement building.

What a scene they were confronted with when they dashed into the house!

Young Agnes in an agony nursing her burns; her mother lying immobile on the floor; and young George standing by, crying and sobbing, helpless to do anything.

One of the neighbours immediately telephoned the

authorities and complained about the danger the children were living in.

A social worker came within half an hour and tried to take the children away from Agnes. However, the children held on tightly to their mother and refused to go. Eventually, the social worker announced that she would get a court order enabling her to put the children into care, and Agnes into a home.

It should be pointed out here that the social worker was acting in what she considered to be the best interests of both Agnes and her children. And it's true that many of the neighbours agreed with her.

Agnes gratefully acknowledges that, in the midst of all these trials, the Lord never forsook her. All the troubles and heartaches which came her way could not sever the link between her and her Saviour.

She says, "When you put your hand of faith in the hand of Jesus there are two currents flowing. One is a current of sorrow flowing from your heart to the heart of Christ. The other is a current of compassion flowing from Him into your life. I did not go unhelped in those days. I had only to reach out and touch my Lord and He would help me. I didn't know how He would do it; where He would do it — or when. But I did know He would do it."

The very next morning, Saturday, the dreaded envelope, containing the court order, arrived. The children were to be taken to the court hearing on Thursday, the 24th, at eleven o'clock and were to be accompanied by a responsible person.

Agnes was in a terrible state and didn't know what to do. All she could do was to cry continually to God for help.

At that moment, in walked Sadie Galloway and Agnes showed her the letter.

Sadie said, "I won't be very long," and out she went again.

Sadie went to the nearest telephone box, called Pastor Kelly, and explained the plight to him. He came immediately and assured Agnes of his support and help. He would go to the court, along with Agnes' doctor, and make whatever appearance he could for her.

They hoped to be able to get the children into a home which would be near enough for them to visit their mother regularly — and this was really the best they could hope for.

The picture didn't look good at all but her friend Sadie was a great source of encouragement to her. On the Sunday she called again to say, "Jesus is still on the throne and He will remember His own. We'll do the praying and let the Lord do the work. He's good at that."

On the following Monday Agnes seemed to be in an even worse state than ever before. In fact, so bad was she, that the home help wanted to send for the doctor but Agnes said no.

Just then two ladies who had been former colleagues in the Salvation Army called to enquire if Agnes lived there. It wasn't usual for Agnes to have visitors but, on this occasion, Betty allowed them to come in to see her. However, she did warn them that, since they hadn't seen her for about eight years, and, since she was so ill, they must expect to see a very different person to the one they knew.

When they came in it was obvious that they were very shocked by what they saw. Instead of trying to communicate with the sick lady and offering her some consolation, they began discussing the tragedy of her case between themselves.

One of them suggested that Agnes had lost her mind and that her understanding was gone; the other ventured to suggest that it would have been much better if the Lord had taken her away from this scene of time.

Agnes sat there hearing all this, but unable to say a word

in response. Every word they uttered was like a knife being plunged into her breast and twisted around.

While the two visitors were still in the house, and still discussing Agnes, Sadie arrived in.

She was so excited! She looked from Agnes to the visitors, and back again.

"Why all the gloom and doom?" she enquired. "I've found the answer to all the problems."

Agnes' heart leaped. She thought someone had offered to give the children a home and said as much to Sadie.

"Oh no, it's not that," said Sadie. "You're going to be healed!"

She was absolutely confident about it. There were no ifs or buts, no mights or maybes. Agnes was going to be healed — and very soon too.

"But," Agnes protsted, "how can I be healed?"

Sadie was quick to tell her.

"God is going to do it. There's a Divine Healing Campaign coming to Paisley Town Hall. Pastor Alex Tee will be the speaker." Sadie's eyes were glittering with excitement. "You go," — she spoke with intense conviction — "and you will be healed!"

Agnes' first reaction was, "Look at me! How could I get there? I can't walk."

By this time Sadie, although full of the excitement of what she believed, was getting a bit exasperated at Agnes' lack of faith.

"Don't worry," she said, "we'll get a taxi."

Again Agnes protested, "But I don't have any money."

Sadie's exasperation was turning to anger.

"Look," she said, "God has a whole lot up in Heaven and if He has to He'll send some down."

At last Agnes seemed to be satisfied that a miracle could take place.

All this time the visitors had stood by quietly, listening to the conversation, but taking no part in it. Now it was their turn to try and put a damper on Sadie's faith.

One of them spoke up and said, "I tried that sort of thing once for a sore back but it was no use. I went to the meeting with a pain and came back home with the same pain."

Her remark had an immediate and dramatic effect on Agnes. In the same way that natural enemies often gang up on a common foe Agnes suddenly found herself defending Sadie's exemplary faith.

Turning to the woman who had complained about the inefficacy of the healing power on her sore back she retorted, "You can't merely try anything belonging to Jesus. Not salvation! — not healing!— not anythng! You either believe it — or you reject it; but you can't say you'll try it."

The lady who made the remark was not to be silenced so easily. "If you believe that why don't you go to the meeting then?"

"I will," said Agnes, "and I'll be healed!"

The Salvation Army lady was determined to have the final say and flung out one last determined challenge. "Come along to the Salvation Army hall then and let's see you after you've been healed." She didn't realise just how soon Agnes would take up that challenge.

10

Release from Despair

After everyone had left Agnes felt so alone and afraid. What had she said? Did she really believe God would heal her? After all, she had asked for healing many times before but it had never happened. Now it seemed as though she would soon be in a home and her children taken from her by order of the court. Would she ever see them again?

By the time her daughter came in from school Agnes was shaking more than ever before. Young Agnes suggested that the doctor should be sent for but Agnes knew that she was beyond the help of any earthly physician. None of the tablets she was taking were of any real benefit either. Unless the "Great Physician" would intervene her case was all but lost.

She decided to crawl through to the bedroom and lie down. As she entered the bedroom she was confronted with an unforgettable sight. The home help had been dusting there earlier that day and had inadvertently left the dressing table mirror at such an angle as to enable Agnes to see herself. The sight that met her eyes was shocking in the extreme.

The first thing that grabbed her attention was he face. It was vacant and expressionless with a mouth that lay open constantly dribbling saliva. As her eyes surveyed the whole scene she looked at her body. It was, in reality, just skin and bone. One arm was twisted and useless while the other pumped up and down as it had now for years. Her legs, which looked as if they were tied to her body, were thin and wasted; and at the top of one of them there was a great big sore which seemed to never heal. It was big enough to put an egg into.

As she gazed at herself in the mirror she wondered how God could ever do anything with such a mess. It looked impossible. Somehow, for the first time since her illness had begun, Agnes felt alone. She had always enjoyed a great sense of the Lord's presence. She had always been able to pray and talk with her Lord on the most intimate terms. But now it seemed as though He was far away and she was forsaken.

As she lay on the bed her daughter pleaded with her to allow her to send for the doctor but Agnes stubbornly resisted.

"Just leave me alone," she said. "And don't bother coming back till morning. I'll be alright. I just want to be alone."

She lay like that until about three o'clock in the morning, struggling with her thoughts and crying to God for help. Then she noticed the Bible lying a little way away on the floor. She crawled over to where it lay and opened it with her mouth. Before she did so she put up another earnest prayer to heaven.

"Please Lord, will you show me that you love me and that you haven't left me. I don't care if you never heal me. It doesn't matter if the children are taken and put into care and I'm not put into hospital. Just as long as you don't leave me. Just as long as you let me know you still love me."

Then her eyes lit on the page of the Bible where it had fallen open and she read a message that was truly from God.

"IS ANY SICK AMONG YOU? LET HIM CALL FOR THE ELDERS OF THE CHURCH; AND LET THEM PRAY OVER HIM, ANOINTING HIM WITH OIL IN THE NAME OF THE LORD: AND THE PRAYER OF FAITH SHALL HEAL THE SICK, AND THE LORD SHALL RAISE HIM UP."—(James Ch. 5 vs. 14 & 15).

Agnes could hardly take in the words yet she knew they were from God.

"Call for the elders of the church." This is what Sadie had been talking about. But was Pastor Tee, the man who was to have the healing service in Paisley Town Hall, an elder? She later discovered that he was.

Then she began to shout and praise the Lord. "Glory to God I'm going to be healed," she cried out. She thought, "If the lady who had sent for the cruelty could see or hear me now she would send for a psychiatrist!"

Somehow Agnes knew God was going to heal her this time. There wasn't a shadow of a doubt in her mind that Jesus was going to make her whole.

Suddenly, she stopped praising God as a certain realisation dawned upon her. This was the early hours of Tuesday morning. The healing meeting in Paisley wasn't till Thursday night but the court was on Thursday morning! If she went to the court in this unhealed state there was no doubt that her children would be taken from her. Furthermore, regardless of when she was healed, it would be much easier to lose her children than to win them back again.

As this agony of truth rushed through her head she began to pray again. "Lord, if I'm still like this when the children go to the court hearing I will lose them. Please, will you heal me before Thursday? Show me what I've got to do Lord."

Then she heard the Lord say to her, "There is a prayer meeting in the Elim Church tonight. If you go to it I will heal you."

Now the Elim Church was right over on the other side of Glasgow and this presented the great problem of actually getting there. What happened next must surely rank high in the annals of sheer human endeavour.

When her home help, Betty, arrived in the morning Agnes asked her if she could take her to the Elim Church that night. However, it was Betty's wedding anniversary and she and a few friends were going out for the evening to celebrate. Regrettably she couldn't help her.

Agnes asked her daughter and son, too, but they were equally unhelpful. "How could you go mum, you can't walk!" they said. Young Agnes went to night school, George to the Sea-Cadets and I suppose they didn't see any purpose in disrupting their normal pattern for what seemed their mother's sudden whim. Agnes understood and never blamed them. But again the Word of God came to her, "You go and you will be healed."

By about five o'clock in the afternoon, when everyone had left the house, Agnes began putting her plan into action.

She had only one coat which, because of her disability, didn't even go on properly — it just sort of hung loosely about her shoulders. But she got it and then struggled for ages to put a hat on too. She crawled to the door, opened the snib with her mouth and then crawled out onto the landing.

It was only then that she realised she lived three stories up in the tenement building. It had been so long since she had been out that she had forgotten about the stairs. What would she do now? There was no way that she could ever negotiate three flights of stairs like a normal person. She crawled over to the edge of them and said a prayer. "Lord, don't let me be hurt too much when I fall down these stairs." And with that she just let herself go over the edge of them.

When she got to the bottom there was a short "close", or passage, to crawl along and then another dozen or so steps from there down to the pavement and the street. The same procedure was adopted for descending these steps too. By the time she got to the street she was black and blue.

Her tumble onto the street alerted the neighbour who had been so anxious about the danger to the children a few days previously when the kettle was knocked over. She obviously had looked out and seen who it was for she called out, "Mrs. Hancock, get back up those stairs. It's time you were in hospital or in a home."

Agnes wondered why she didn't come after her immediately but later she found out the reason. The lady in question had just bathed her new baby and then put her 18-months-old son into the bath to play while she dried and dressed the baby. It was impossible for her, just at the moment, to go after Agnes. It seemed as if God had put a chain on her that night so that she couldn't stop Agnes getting to the meeting.

It was a pouring wet, miserable night and as Agnes crawled slowly along the pavement she must have been the most pitiful of sights. Her coat trailed on the ground, gathering mud and wet as she moved along. People stared, some in amazement, some in horror, some in disbelief.

Eventually, she got to the bus-stop and somehow managed to get on board. She had prayed that the conductress would be upstairs and she was. This meant that she could sit in that little cubby hole under the stairs where parcels were normally kept. By the time the conductress saw her she was so wet, miserable and dirty that she took pity on her and allowed her to stay.

Agnes asked the conductress to let her off at Eglinton Toll. Of course, when the bus arrived there, Agnes couldn't get off by herself so the conductress called up the stairs for someone to help her. Two men and the bus-driver came to see what all the commotion was about and they lifted Agnes off the bus and propped her against the wall of a nearby pub.

Agnes sat there, in the pouring rain, for about an hour and a half calling out, "Would somebody please help me?" Again, most of the people passing by looked at her with dismay and pity but no one came to her assistance. I suppose they thought she was drunk.

Then, once again, the hand of God's providence worked on her behalf. Another lady, Mrs. Baxter, who had been going to the same prayer meeting in the Elim Church happened to be a little late. When she got to the door of the church a voice seemed to say to her, "You're too late for the meeting. Don't go in. Just go back and get the bus home again."

She wasn't sure whether this was the voice of God or the voice of the Devil but anyhow, she obeyed it. Even as she went back to wait for the bus she kept wondering where the voice could have come from.

When she got to the bus-stop she was no longer in any doubt. There sat this woman against the wall of the pub and she was crying out for help. Surely this was why God had sent her back.

She bent down over Agnes and when she saw the face and realised who it was she almost shrank back in shock. "Mrs. Hancock, what are you doing so far away from home; and how did you get here?" she exclaimed.

Agnes told her of how the Lord promised to heal her and of how important it was to get to the church that night. Mrs. Baxter was sympathetic and understanding and said, "Well, let's get to the church before it closes." With that she stepped into the middle of the road and held up the traffic while Agnes crawled across to the other side. By now it was twenty minutes past eight.

The last short distance to the church hall seemed to take an age but Agnes was buoyed up by the assurance that God was going to heal her. When they got to the church Mrs. Baxter pushed open the door and Agnes crawled in.

The prayer meeting was already in progress and one dear saint of God was, at that moment, leading the whole group, audibly, in prayer. Excitement and anticipation were welling up within Agnes and she thought this man would never finish his prayer. She just couldn't wait so she called out, "Would you please stop praying until I'm healed; you can all pray after that." The man who was praying stopped at once.

Pastor Kelly quickly intervened. "Our sister has come for prayer and I want you all to pray as you never have prayed before. But first, we're going to sing a chorus."

Agnes interjected, "No singing, no choruses until I'm healed. God has told me to call for the elders of the church and to have them pray for me." And then in what might have seemed like insolence or brashness but what, in reality, was just her way of making absolutely sure she was fulfilling all God's conditions for this healing miracle she asked, "Do you have elders or will deacons do?"

Pastor Kelly assured her that they did have elders — and deacons — and that they were all there at the meeting. Then he called them around and they knelt down on the floor beside Agnes. Pastor Kelly took the oil and anointed her head in the name of the Lord Jesus and prayed for the healing of her body.

Immediately something amazing happened! First her arm, which had pumped uncontrollably for years, became still and motionless. Quickly Agnes put her hands to her face to find if anything had happened there. To her delight her face was normal. The mouth was no longer distorted nor did it continually dribble saliva anymore. Agnes thought, "If my hand is all right and my face has returned to normal, then my legs must be O.K. too." She jumped up and for the first time in five years was able to stand without falling over.

The scene that followed can hardly be described. Agnes began calling out, "I'm healed! I'm healed! Praise God you've healed me!" Soon everyone was shouting; crying; laughing and praising God with her.

Agnes Hancock, the helpless cripple, had been wonderfully healed. A miracle had taken place in her life!

11

The New Creature

On the day before she had been healed Agnes had been visited by two nurses. They had done a number of checks on her health and had also weighed her. They found her to be seriously under weight, a mere five stone two lbs., in fact. (72 lbs.) However, when the Lord healed her he restored her body completely to normal and that meant correcting her weight also. Within the space of ten minutes her weight increased from that skeletal five stone two lbs. to a healthy nine stones. (126 lbs.)

Agnes often says that what took place was unbelievable. There was a touch of humour there too, for as she watched her limbs and body filling up she just had to cry out, "Not too much Lord!"

Strange as it may seem Agnes did not stay in the church for very long. You and I would have imagined her to remain for hours praising God and giving thanks; meeting the people and receiving their good wishes. But she didn't. She excused herself almost immediately and left to go home to her children. Before she did so she asked the people to thank the Lord for her and then, promised, "I'll come back another night and thank Him myself."

What a different person she was as she made her way

back to the bus-stop. Her legs now strong and powerful; her face perfectly featured and her skin smooth; her arms and hands working normally and absolutely under control.

Just as she got to the bus-stop the bus was moving off. Without hesitation she broke into a sprint, caught up with the accelerating vehicle and jumped on. As she did so the conductress appeared on the platform. Agnes, thrilled with her new found athletic ability, said to her quite enthusiastically, "Did you see the way I ran and jumped onto the bus there?"

The conductress, ignorant of the greater event which had just taken place in the Elim church, retorted sharply, "You'll do that once too often!"

Agnes began to explain how she had just been healed. But the conductress, looking I suppose at the outward appearance of ragged and dirty coat, was unimpressed and, with a voice full of unbelief, simply said, "That's good, go and sit down."

Agnes took a seat near the door of the bus and beside a man who was reading the newspaper. After a few moments she was again unable to hold her tongue. She just had to tell people. So she nudged this man with her elbow and said, "I've just been healed. God did it. It's wonderful isn't it?" The gentleman was equally unimpressed.

When she eventually got off the bus Agnes ran all the way back to her tenement building. The first person she met was the neighbour who lived in the bottom house and who had been unable to follow her because of her pre-occupation with her children.

She stopped Agnes and said, "Excuse me, but have you seen a cripple woman anywhere?"

Overjoyed at what had happened to her and unable to suppress her natural mischievous spirit Agnes replied, "Oh, you won't be seeing her anymore."

"But why," said the neighbour, "is she dead."

Agnes couldn't keep the secret any longer. "I'm sorry you've been so worried, she said, "I'm the one you're looking for."

"Oh no, but you don't understand," protested the neighbour, "Mrs. Hancock's a cripple. She can't walk. It's getting dark and I've been looking everywhere for her. I'm so worried about her."

Agnes replied, "Yes, I do understand, because I am that cripple. But God has just healed me."

At this point the neighbour seemed to recognise the old coat. Taking hold of Agnes by the arm she pulled her into the close to where there was a light, had a good look at her and exclaimed, "My God, it is you!" Hardly able to utter another word she ran for the lady in the house next door. "Look! Look!" she cried. "It's the cripple from upstairs. She says she's healed."

The second neighbour was equally thunderstruck. Both of them stood there amazed — and frightened at the same time.

Agnes began to relate the story of her wonderful healing, while someone else ran to tell more neighbours. Just as it must have been in Bible times when Jesus performed his miracles, the news spread like wildfire. In a short time the house where Agnes lived was packed with people who had come to see the miracle lady.

Several members of the press turned up too. They were anxious to cover this amazing event and one of them even offered Agnes £150.00 for an exclusive story. However, Agnes could not sell anything that the Lord had done for her and all the reporters were given the story together. It appeared next day in many of the newspapers.

In the middle of all this Agnes' daughter arrived home. As she came into the house and saw all the people she was worried at first that something serious had happened her mother. And then she saw her. At first she stood transfixed, hardly able to believe the evidence of her eyes. Then she ran and hugged her mother asking, "How did it happen?"

When she heard of what the Lord had done she promised, "One day I will be a nurse and help sick people. I'll try to help pay back what God has done for my mother." At 17 she kept that childhood promise and is still nursing to this day.

The reaction of Agnes' son George was quite different and very sad. First there was the look of disbelief. Could this really be his mother? Yes, it was. Then there was the questioning attitude. "Do you mean to say that God could have healed you years ago and yet He allowed you to suffer so?" It seemed that in a moment of time his child-like faith had been shattered. All these years later Agnes still prays for his return to the Lord and for household salvation.

It was about three o'clock in the morning before the house was finally cleared and everyone got to bed. Agnes was up again early and for the first time for years, helped the children get ready for school and saw them out. She told them to be sure to snib the door this morning because she wanted to go and answer it when Betty came.

In a little while she heard Betty trying to let herself in, then fearing they had all overslept and the children would be late for school, calling through the letter box.

Agnes went to the door, opened it and assured Betty that the children were already on their way. Betty stood there looking at Agnes for a few moments and then she said, "Who are you?" Before Agnes had time to answer she burst out with, "It can't be!" Then, "It is you — isn't it."

Agnes said, "Come in Betty. I'll get you a cup of tea this morning, you seem to need it."

When Betty got over the initial shock of seeing Agnes walking about as normal she sat while Agnes related the whole wonderful story of how the Lord had healed her.

Betty was deeply touched, so touched in fact, that she wanted to get to know the Lord for herself. It was Agnes' great joy to point her to the Saviour who could perform the even greater miracle of healing the disease of sin and setting her free from the bonds of iniquity.

As both of them sat there crying for joy Betty exclaimed, "I don't know why I'm so happy! I've just lost my job; you won't need me anymore now." And then as she thought about it she continued, "I don't even know if I should stay this morning. What should we do about that?"

Agnes suggested that she should go down to the telephone-box at the corner of the street and contact her office. They would know what to do.

When she phoned the office Betty said, "This is Betty Stevenson." Then she started to cry. "Mrs. Hancock doesn't need me anymore."

The supervisor, who was well acquainted with Agnes' case, anticipated the worst and said, "Oh dear, when did she die?"

When Betty explained that, far from being dead, Agnes was better than she had been for years and had been healed the previous night, she got an altogether different response to what she expected.

The supervisor knew that she had been out the night before celebrating her wedding anniversary. She was convinced that Betty had been over-indulging at the wine and was still suffering the after effects, so she gave Betty firm and definite instructions.

"You know, Betty, it's instant dismissal if you're drunk on the job. You go straight back to that house and wait there until I come. I'll be there right away. And whatever you do, don't upset Mrs. Hancock."

Betty waited — and the supervisor came.

When she walked in she was visibly shocked. "I don't believe it. It is you isn't it?" she said, addressing Agnes. "I think it's me that needs a drink." After a few minutes she went off to tell two other supervisors, Sister Claypole and Sister Donald.

A short time later Sister Donald arrived at the house to see for herself and commented, "If this doesn't make people think of the Lord, what will?" She also suggested that Betty should be allowed to stay for the rest of the day to help Agnes cope with the vast numbers of people who were calling and to give her a hand at answering all the mail that was pouring in.

Just with that the insurance man called for his weekly payment. He said, "Good morning," to Agnes and then looked all around the room for the invalid.

"Where is she?" he said.

"Who are you looking for?" enquired Agnes.

"Mrs. Hancock, the lady who's ill. Where is she?" he replied.

Agnes couldn't keep a straight face any longer. She laughed and said, "It's me. I got healed last night."

The poor man was dumbfounded. He looked at Agnes, then at Betty; who nodded her head and said, "Yes, it's Mrs. Hancock all right;" then back to Agnes again. He left the house in a daze but he had every intention of being back before the day was out.

After he had gone Agnes decided to pay her doctor a visit. When she checked in at the receptionist's desk she was asked, "Are you on the doctor's list?"

Agnes replied that she was and that her name was Mrs. Hancock. The receptionist checked the file and then said, "I'm sorry, you can't be that lady. She's a cripple and hasn't been out for years."

Agnes explained how she had been healed the night before and that she only wanted two minutes with the doctor to tell him so. The receptionist wasn't sure whether to believe her or not but eventually made a bargain with her.

"If I let you go in to see the doctor will you leave the door open so that I can hear." Agnes agreed.

When she walked into the surgery the doctor was sitting

73

at his desk, writing, and wasn't aware of who had come in. Agnes said quite chirpily, "Good morning doctor, how are you?"

He looked up at Agnes and a puzzled expression came to his face. He looked again and said, "For a moment I thought you were someone else, but that's impossible."

"Yes," said Agnes. "With man it is impossible. But with God all things are possible. That's why I'm here this morning."

The doctor looked at her again and by this time his mouth hung open.

"You are her, aren't you" he said, not using her name as if in recognition that she would know who he was talking about.

"Yes, it's me," said Agnes. "I was healed last night," and she told him the whole story.

"I just can't believe that this is happening" said the doctor. "Only that you are sitting there I wouldn't believe it. How ...? Why ...? I don't know." He couldn't even complete his own questions.

When he had settled a little he told Agnes that just a few minutes ago he had received the report from the nurses who had visited her the previous morning. It said that she weighed only five stone and two lbs. (72 lbs.)

"Let's see," said the doctor, "you look a bit more than that this morning. Stand on the scales here."

Agnes now weighed nine stones exactly. (126 lbs.) The doctor was amazed. That amazement was shared by all the doctors and professors at Glasgow Royal Infirmary later that same morning. Her own doctor was so impressed by what he had seen that he cancelled surgery for the rest of the morning and drove her there in his own car so that they all could see what a transformation had taken place.

Some of the learned men said it might last a week. Others thought it could continue for a few months, maybe even a year. But all were sure it would come back again and, when it did, it would be much worse. All, that is, except for one man, her own professor. He said, "Let her enjoy this experience. Whatever has happened God has done it for her. Just leave her alone."

12

Provision and Power

In all this there was one slight note of sadness. Agnes' friend Sadie Galloway, the one who had first assured her that she would be healed, had missed the whole thing. She had been away on Tuesday evening, trying to organise a lift for the Thursday meeting with Pastor Tee.

Pastor Kelly telephoned her on the Tuesday night after the miracle had taken place and given her the great news. Of course, she was delighted. When Agnes arrived back from the hospital late on the Wednesday morning, Sadie was waiting for her. After the whole story had been rehearsed once more, she too, joined in the praising and giving of thanks. Then, quite out of the blue, she sprung a great surprise on Agnes.

"Don't take off that coat," she said. "This is the last time you'll be wearing it. You'll need a new one now to show off your new body."

With that she ushered Agnes out of the house and down the town to a big warehouse. On the way Agnes protested that she didn't have any money. How could she afford a new coat?

"Who said anything about money?" replied Sadie, and led Agnes onward on their errand.

When they got into the warehouse the sales assistant brought out a number of coats but they were all rejected as unsuitable. The trouble was that the assistant was looking at Agnes' old coat and was judging the price range from that. Consequently, she brought only the cheapest ones. This didn't satisfy Sadie who told the girl so. Finally, a beautiful blue coat, which Agnes knew must have been very expensive, was brought.

"That's the one," announced Sadie. "You'll be working for God now and only the best is good enough for Him." She paid for the coat and out they both came; Sadie, rejoicing in what the Lord had enabled her to do; Agnes, in what the Lord had done.

Even today Agnes realises that Sadie was, by no means, a woman of substance. But she was generous with whatever the Lord gave her and never wanted for anything after her kindness to Agnes.

When Agnes arrived home with the new coat, who was waiting for her but the two insurance men. The one who called regularly every week and, along with him, his inspector. It was quite some time before the inspector could speak. When he did it was with tear filled eyes.

"I can hardly believe my eyes," he said. "I will never doubt God anymore."

Then he confessed how that, as a young man, he had given his life to the Lord. Through the years, however, he had allowed the world to come in and take control and the things of God had been given a back seat in his life.

"Do you think He will forgive me?" he asked.

What a joy it was for Agnes to kneel in prayer with both of these men as they sought Jesus again.

And how amusing, in a sense, to hear them ask if she wanted to be insured now as there was no longer any hindrance.

Next morning, the Thursday, was the dreaded day of the court case. However, now that Agnes had been healed there was no longer the same dread.

In the court the magistrate asked who was representing the Hancock children. Agnes spoke up and said that she was. He then enquired what relationship she was to these children and when Agnes said that she was their mother, he was quite puzzled.

Turning to the social worker he queried, "But I thought this woman was a cripple?"

The social worker was equally puzzled and couldn't explain why Mrs. Hancock stood there looking so normal.

The magistrate asked what this was all about and Agnes explained that she had been healed of her sickness a couple of nights previously.

The social worker suggested that it would be a good idea to take the children into care, for at least a little while, in case there would be a recurrence of the problem.

The magistrate, however, didn't share her opinion. He said, "She looks healthy enough to me. I'm going to let her take the children home with her. But keep an eye on her condition and if there's any deterioration, bring her back to me again." Then turning to Agnes he said, "You take the children with you, keep trusting in your God, and may you all be very happy. I don't think you'll ever be back again."

Agnes left the court with joy in her heart and praise on her lips. Another great burden had been lifted from her shoulders.

The remarkable events which had taken place in her life brought Agnes a new found popularity. This was only to be expected for, after all, her story had been in all the papers and was, literally, the talk of the town. She was inundated with requests and invitations from churches and fellowships all over the country, to come and tell what had happened.

The very first meeting she attended was the one in Paisley Town Hall where Pastor Tee was holding the divine healing services. As had been planned, she went on the Thursday night, but it was to tell Pastor Tee what a great miracle had already been wrought in her life.

On the following Sunday evening she was at Pastor Kelly's Elim church and telling a packed audience there of what the Lord had done for her.

After that she travelled all over the country, to meetings large and small, telling her story.

Through what had happened to Agnes many lives were changed. Indeed, even as the healing miracle was taking place the Lord was working in at least one young heart.

Tommy Burns was a Roman Catholic lad and had been brought to the prayer meeting in Elim church by his mother, who had been saved just a short time before.

You can imagine the dramatic effect the healing service had upon him. It convinced him that here was the power of God at work, as he had never seen it. He immediately gave his heart to the Lord and then dedicated his young life to Him. Eventually, he became a pastor in the Elim assemblies and, at the time of writing, is pastoring a church in Aberdeen, Scotland.

He says, "The impact of that meeting will never leave me. To see the hand of God at work in such a fashion is something I will never forget. It has made me realise throughout my life the wonder working power of the Lord Jesus Christ."

Amy Jack, who was just a very young girl then, was also in the meeting that night. Today she is the wife of Elim pastor, Ian Waddell, and living in Bishop Auckland, in the north of England. Both their lives were very much influenced by that wonderful event and they often accompanied Agnes on her engagements throughout the country.

Tuesday the 29th September, just one week after she was healed, was another red letter day in Agnes' life.

She was invited to have tea with a Mrs. Porter, who had also been in the meeting the night she was healed.

When she arrived at Mrs. Porter's the tea was already prepared so they immediately sat down at the table. Agnes was asked to give thanks and bowing her head along with the others started to pray.

She only managed to utter the opening word, "Lord ....," when suddenly the Holy Spirit came upon her in a remarkable way. She received a new power — a power which she had never known before — and as she continued to pray she seemed to be lifted out of the immediate surroundings to experience a closeness to God that hitherto had been unknown. So powerful and extraordinary was this experience that, even today, she finds it difficult to describe.

She believes that that "baptism of the Holy Spirit" is the source of all the strength and power she has known since then.

13

The Enemy Fights Back

A lot of people still ask Agnes what eventually happened to her children so perhaps a mention of them here would be in order.

It was pointed out earlier that, on the night Agnes was healed, her daughter had dedicated her life to the service of others. When she was seventeen young Agnes began nursing training and, in due course, qualified. During the time she was training she met a young man called Norman Henderson, also a Christian, and in April 1966 they were married.

George also got married, to Ann Letson, in December 1972.

Today Agnes is very proud of her four grandchildren: Anne, Irene, George and Jacqueline. Both families are very happy and Agnes looks forward to her frequent visits to their homes.

Shortly after she was healed Agnes became a member of Pastor Kelly's church. Sunday after Sunday would find her in her place, enjoying the ministry of the word and supporting God's work with her prayers. She constantly gives thanks for those happy days with the fellowship of other believers and the faithfulness of God's servant.

However, in due course, Pastor Kelly reached retirement age and, after twenty-five years service to the one congregation, decided to devote more time to looking after his ailing wife.

The church had a farewell service for him and, as part of it, Agnes was asked to pay tribute to him. She decided to do so in the form of a poem:

> *"I would like to pay tribute,*
> *Though not without tears,*
> *To our pastor who is leaving*
> *After twenty-five years.*
>
> *As the boy preacher, when young,*
> *He was lively and keen.*
> *He had his first church*
> *When just seventeen.*
>
> *We all love our pastor*
> *From the Emerald Isle.*
> *He gives a warm handshake*
> *And a real friendly smile.*
>
> *They say you can tell an Irishman*
> *From village or town*
> *But when he opens his mouth*
> *You can always see down.*
>
> *That Irish brogue of our pastor,*
> *(He hasn't lost it you'll note)*
> *You'd think it was just yesterday*
> *He came off the boat.*
>
> *He preached a full gospel,*
> *Whether to women or men,*
> *Emphasising the need*
> *To be born again.*

As for all the young people,
  The short and the tall,
And the little children
  He sure loved them all.

He kindly visited our homes
  When sick, or in need.
As soon as he knew
  He came at full speed.

We liked his bright humour,
  He could make us all laugh.
So much that at times
  Folk might think we were daft.

He could sing as well as preach,
  We all know that's true,
But which he was best at
  We'll leave that to you.

Yes he's been a great pastor
  And never would grieve us.
Except that now
  He is going to leave us.

We've heard many preachers
  From 'radio' or 'telly';
But none that was better
  Than our own Pastor Kelly.

But now it's good-bye
  And we feel we could greet
But our good-bye's not forever
  In heaven we'll meet.

God bless you dear pastor;
For retirement you're set
But your long faithful service
We'll never forget."

The new pastor at the Elim church was Stephen Hilliard and, as he took up the work, the Lord continued His blessing.

Shortly after this Agnes had to go into hospital for, what seemed, a simple ear test. Her general health was good at the time; her only problem being a touch of deafness in one ear. It was quite a shock, then, to be told that an immediate operation would be necessary.

Agnes just couldn't understand what was happening but, when her daughter who worked at the hospital, saw the X-rays she advised her mother to agree. Within one hour of being admitted to the hospital the operation was being performed.

Next morning, when the effects of the anaesthetic had worn off, Agnes was given a gentle reprimand because she hadn't told the doctors of her history of Parkinson's disease.

Agnes was quick to tell the doctors that, although she had suffered from Parkinson's disease a number of years ago, she had been healed and was sure that it would never re-occur.

The doctor wasn't to be so easily put off. "I'm afraid," he said, "there has been a re-occurrence of your sickness. Look at your hand."

Sure enough, her hand was shaking, just as it would in the early stages of Parkinson's disease.

Two weeks later, suffering from loss of balance which the ear operation had done nothing to mend, she was transferred from the Western Infirmary to the neurology department of the Southern General Hospital.

One day, when the professor and students were making their rounds, the students were asked for their opinion as to what was wrong with Agnes. Some of the students suggested that this was the early stages of Parkinson's disese and, as evidence, pointed to the shaking arm.

When Agnes heard this she sat on the trembling arm and asserted, "It's not shaking."

The students, understandably, laughed at what seemed to them a very blatant, but rather poor, cover up job.

However, the professor intervened quite swiftly. Pulling a file from the batch he had with him and presenting it to the students with an air of authority he said, "Read that!"

The file contained the full report of Agnes' case, from the time she was first diagnosed as having Parkinson's disease, up to, and including, her healing.

The professor went on, "When did you ever see Parkinson's disease lying dormant for a day, never mind for fourteen years?" Then, as they moved off he continued, "Before you laugh at anything study the facts."

Agnes couldn't believe and wouldn't believe that a sickness, which God had taken away, would ever return to her. As she puzzled over this Pastor Hilliard came to visit her. She asked him to bring Jack Burns, one of the men who had originally prayed for her, to the hospital and requested that they both anoint her with oil and pray again for her healing.

Pastor Hilliard didn't agree right away because he couldn't admit to having the faith needed to fall in with Agnes' request. He walked out into the grounds of the hospital and turned the matter over in his mind for some time. Then, returning to Agnes, he announced that he would do as she requested.

They did anoint Agnes, praying that this sickness, whatever it was, would leave her body. However, nothing happened immediately.

Agnes firmly believes that, "All things work together for good to them that Love God," and this sudden apparent re-occurrence of an old trouble was no exception. She believes that whatever this sickness was, it was designed to make sure that she would be in the Southern General Hospital just at this time.

On the opposite side of the ward lay a young woman who had suffered a broken back. It was expected that she would never walk again and she was about to be discharged, with a special bed which would make life more comfortable for her at home.

When the professor and students left the ward this woman, her name was Ann, called Agnes over and asked her to pray for her. Agnes had already related the story of how she had been anointed with oil, prayed for by the elders, and healed.

Agnes was just pulling up her chair beside Ann's bed and preparing to pray with her when Ann said, "You were anointed with oil, please do the same for me."

Agnes didn't have any oil but a young Christian nurse, who overheard the conversation, appeared a short time later with a small bottle and popped it into the pocket of Agnes' dressing gown. It was almond oil.

Agnes anointed Ann with the oil and prayed for her to be healed. At first nothing seemed to happen, although this fact did not dampen Ann's faith. She was quite convinced she would be healed and, when her husband John arrived shortly after, told him so.

The physiotherapist was in the process of showing John how to work the special bed when Ann said, "My big toe is moving!"

The physiotherapist said, "Nonsense, my dear, it's just a nerve working."

Ann was adamant, "My toe IS moving. I can feel it!"

The physiotherapist wasn't to be convinced and insisted that it was just as she had said, a nervous reaction.

After a little while John intervened. "Don't you think it might be a good idea to remove the blankets and have a look?"

Eventually, the physiotherapist was persuaded that this would be the thing to do. She removed the blankets to reveal Ann's feet and she and John peered down to look for movement in the toe.

Just then Ann's voice was heard, "See! I told you! My toe is moving!"

At the same time, out of the corner of his eye John could see Ann's hand, with a finger pointing, coming into the picture. He turned to look and, behold, Ann was not only pointing, she was sitting upright in the bed. Imagine the amazement of all who were there seeing, not just a toe wiggling, but its owner sitting upright for the first time since the accident which had broken her back.

Two days later she walked out of the hospital carrying her two-year-old child in her arms for the first time.

14

The Wheelchair

A few days after Ann's wonderful healing Agnes left hospital too, and went to stay with her daughter and son-in-law. Her daughter had already arranged for them all to go to the W.E.C. (Worldwide Evangelisation Crusade Missionary Society) Conference held at Kilcreggan in the East of Scotland.

Kilcreggan is a beautiful place; away from all the hustle and bustle of city life with fresh, clear air and beautiful views over the Clyde.

The spacious grounds, with the big house dominating the whole scene, are an ideal place for relaxing walks and quiet meditation. It's also the perfect starting point for longer walks along the shores of Gare Loch and Loch Long.

It's interesting to note that the road which runs along above the grounds is said to be the one which inspired Sir Harry Lauder to write, "Keep right on to the end of the road."

There are also pleasant boat trips from Kilcreggan harbour, to such romantic sounding places as Dunoon, Rothesay, Largs and other points on the Clyde. In fact, one of these boat trips features in this story.

Agnes' daughter had planned to take the whole family,

including her mother, for a day on the Clyde. By this time Agnes was confined to a wheel-chair, so her daughter was very keen that her mother would accompany them, not only for the good of her health, but also so that she could keep an eye on her safety. However, Agnes declined to go, insisting instead, on staying behind so that she could spend time alone with the Lord.

She really wanted to sort out the business of her present illness, once and for all. Was the Lord going to heal her again, or was she to be left in this wheel-chair for the rest of her life?

As soon as the boat had pulled away from the shore, Agnes began putting her new plan into action.

First, she managed to negotiate the chair across the grounds to where a blind man, Mr. Buchanan, was sitting basket weaving. Then, she asked him to undo the special strap which kept her in the chair.

This had been fitted because of her persistent attempts to leave the chair and the fact that she kept falling and doing herself injury.

. Mr. Buchanan did manage to undo the safety strap and Agnes then steered the chair over to a quiet part of the grounds and behind a big tree.

She sat there for a long time considering her whole situation, turning it over in her mind and silently praying for the Lord's help and guidance. Then she began to quote, out loud, from 1st John Ch. 5 verses 14 & 15:

> *"And this is the confidence that we have in him, that, if we ask anything according to his will, he heareth us: And if we know that he hear us, whatsoever we ask, we know that we have the petitions that we desired of him."*

On the strength of those words, and in the belief that she was going to be healed, she stood up; in the name of Jesus.

And she really did stand up this time! There was no wavering, no shaking, and no falling over again. She stood; she walked; she ran — all in the name of Jesus.

The wheel-chair was taken back to the chalet, folded up and put away, never to be used again. She went for a walk in the grounds and, as she made her way along, met a man who asked her if she would like to take part in a game of putting they were playing that evening. Agnes had no hesitation in agreeing and her name was jotted down.

It should be pointed out that at meal times, Agnes was transferred from the wheel-chair to an arm-chair. This left more room at the table for others, and for serving the meals too.

At tea time that evening Agnes was sitting at the table, in her usual arm-chair, when her daughter and family walked in. Of course, they suspected nothing and took their places at the table as if everything was still as it had been when they left. Just then someone began to read out the names of those who would be playing in the putting match that night and, at the top of the list, was read out the name of Agnes Hancock.

"There must be some mistake," said her daughter, "my mother can't play putting!"

"Yes I can," interrupted Agnes, "God has healed me once again. I'm all right."

Agnes had a great time that night at the putting match although she can't remember who won.

This was the summer of 1977 and when Agnes returned to Glasgow she took up the work of the Lord with fresh interest and renewed zeal. Meetings were held regularly in her house at Drumchapel where many sought the Lord for salvation and others were healed of their sicknesses.

But there was to be no settling down for her and no staying put either. A letter on its way from Belfast would see to that.

15

If you ever go across the Sea . . . . .

Ernest Yates served on the Irish executive of the Elim churches for a number of years, and he and his wife had been at Kilcreggan when Agnes had been healed the second time. So moved was he by what he had seen, that he was constrained to invite Agnes over to N. Ireland for some meetings.

Agnes accepted and shortly afterwards found herself in Ulster, going the rounds of the Elim churches, the Assemblies of God and some Mission Halls.

What was meant to be a 'one-off' visit turned out to be the forerunner to the next chapter in her life and ministry. Speaking one night in Berlin Street Mission she reminded people that it was nearby in Sugarfield Street that God had first called her to be a Salvation Army officer. And then quite unconsciously she added, "He could very well call me back to Northern Ireland again."

As she left the service a woman asked her where she would be speaking the next evening. Agnes told her, "Ballymena".

The following night, as she left the Elim church in Ballymena, the same woman appeared and pressed an envelope into her hand. Agnes thought it contained money and, believing that the woman was more in need of it than she was, told her so. After a little discussion the woman pointed out that what she had given Agnes was a Northern Ireland Housing Executive application form.

It wouldn't be right to say that Agnes was flabbergasted, but she did give serious thought as to why anyone should think that she needed such a form. And she said as much.

The woman, however, was adamant. "You'll need it if you're going to live over here."

The conversation ended there, but on the way home, Agnes showed Ernie Yates the form and asked him what he thought about it. Ernie suggested that it didn't much matter what he thought about it. More to the point was, what would her daughter and son think about it?

On the following Sunday morning, as he was introducing her to the congregation of Bethesda Elim Church, in Belfast, Pastor Richard Christie announced that he had a message from God for Agnes. It would appear that he didn't understand the full import of the message but he gave it anyway.

"You're to fill in whatever form you have and get it to the place concerned, so that God's will might be fulfilled in your life."

Agnes was returning to Glasgow the following day, and so had to make a decision fairly quickly. She made the whole thing a matter of earnest prayer and decided to fill in the form and submit it to the Housing Executive. At the same time she laid out a fleece before the Lord. She would know it was God's will for her to move to Belfast if she was given a house with two, or more, bedrooms.

The Housing Executive had no difficulty in providing a one bedroom house, but two bedrooms, for someone who in their estimation didn't need them, was quite something else. Agnes would have to go on a waiting list.

The following spring a suitable three bedroom house

became available, and at Easter Agnes moved lock, stock and barrel to Belfast.

The moving is a story by itself.

This was 1979, and Belfast was continually in the news. Street rioting, bombings, gun-fire and murder grabbed the headlines every day of the week. Because of all this, Agnes' family wasn't too happy about her decision to move across the Irish Sea and didn't really offer her much help.

Added to that was the sad fact that one of Agnes' lifelong friends in the Salvation Army had lost her life as a result of terrorist bombing. Maimie Thompson was in the process of salvaging musical instruments from the Salvation Army hall when a bomb went off, killing her instantly. Her husband Sam, was also badly injured.

However, Agnes was not to be put off so easily, especially when she believed that she was following God's will.

Removals to Ulster were expensive, and when you've little or no money, they seem impossible. The cheapest estimate was a staggering £270. Agnes didn't have a penny saved but she had heard of people getting a loan from the bank and thought it was worth a try. She didn't have a bank account but, nonetheless, she had no hesitation in walking into the nearest Bank of Scotland and asking for the manager.

Sitting in the manager's office she explained her position. She was moving to Ireland to work for God and needed a small loan to enable her to get her furniture over there. The manager asked if he could see her bank book, and when Agnes told him she didn't have such a thing he began to make enquiries about how her family felt about this move. When Agnes admitted that her family wasn't at all in favour of the idea the manager quietly suggested that she ought to see a doctor or a social worker. We'll leave it to your imagination to decide what was really going through his mind.

Next morning the telephone rang at five o'clock. It was Pastor Christie who began by asking Agnes why she had kept him and his wife awake all night. He had sensed that there was something troubling Agnes and decided that she needed comforting.

"Why are you worrying?" he said. "Look at what Peter did!"

After he had hung up, Agnes began thinking about Peter and what he had done all those years ago. But the thought of walking across the Irish Sea pulling her furniture behind her didn't really appeal to her. However, it did give her a bit of a chuckle in the middle of a rather worrying time.

Pastor Christie phoned again at ten o'clock that same morning. He said, "I want you to go down to the Bank of Scotland. There's one quite near where you live."

Agnes told him she had been there the day before but hadn't been too well received.

Pastor Christie suggested, as tactfully as possible, that he thought it would be better if she would just walk with God instead of running before Him. He also explained that provision for all her need had already been made with the bank, and that she would find £300 waiting there for her. The money had been made available through the generosity of Pastor Christie, Jack Wylie and Keith Ayton.

And so it was back to the same Bank of Scotland, and the same cautious manager.

This time his attitude was completely different and evidenced his obvious amazement at what had taken place in the short space of twenty-four hours. No one had told Pastor Christie how much was needed; not even that there was a need. And yet the right amount of money had been deposited, with the right bank, at the right time.

An added blessing was the fact that both her son George, and her daughter Agnes became reconciled to their mother's departure to Ireland. They both called to wish her well for the journey and her daughter even decided to go with her to keep her company on the voyage.

And so the great move, back to the land of her childhood, was undertaken.

Agnes Hancock was now 61 years old, yet she had no hesitation in making this journey. She was absolutely confident that the Lord had opened up the way before her, and that he would undertake for all that lay ahead. Only the Lord was to know the coming years were to be the most fruitful and blessed of all her life.

16

In Belfast

Agnes' new address was in the Oldpark area of North Belfast.

Moving in presented a few problems which were a worry at the time. The furniture arrived much later than was promised, and a number of pieces were broken but, with the help of a couple of Christian friends, whom the Lord sent along at just the right time, everything was more or less in order before nightfall.

Next morning when she was out in the garden a man who was passing by stopped to talk to her.

"Why have you come to such a place as this?" he enquired.

Agnes replied that she was there because she felt that was the place God wanted her to be. The man wanted to know more and asked what kind of work she was involved in. When Agnes told him that she spoke at meetings, he asked if she would speak at one for him the following Thursday. It turned out that he was the local Belfast city missionary. And so, she had her very first engagement to speak in Belfast, the day after she arrived.

A little later that day she noticed a woman holding on to the gate. She seemed to be in some sort of pain and appeared to be taking a rest. Agnes went out and spoke to her, enquiring what the trouble was. The woman moaned, "It's just this old back of mine. It gives me a lot of trouble."

Agnes offered to pray for her, saying that the Lord could take the pain away. She brought her in, sat her down, and read from James Ch. 5 verses 14 & 15. Then, anointing her with oil, prayed for her. They spent some time together in conversation and then the lady made to go. When she was about half way to the gate she suddenly realised that the pain was gone and began to speak her praise to the Lord. Thus the first contact had been reached and blessed in Ulster. But the outcome was to be far greater.

This was Saturday, and that same evening the annual conference of the Elim churches was being held in Belfast. Pastor Christie thought it would be an ideal place for Agnes to meet many of the local pastors, and a good opportunity for them to book her for meetings in their churches.

Agnes could hardly believe her eyes when she walked into this hall packed with men. There wasn't another woman in the place. However, she was persuaded to stay, and at the interval her diary was taken from her. When she got it back, it was completely filled with bookings for the next year.

At this point Agnes decided it was time to go, and left the meeting with the intention of going home. When she got outside, however, it suddenly dawned on her that she had no idea of her new address. She remembered that Mrs. Yates lived at a place called Silverstream, and that the bus which took her there passed along the Shankill Road. She thought, "If I can get to the Shankill, perhaps I'll see a bus going in the Silverstream direction, and possibly I'll be able to find where Mrs. Yates lives."

The fact that she didn't go back into the hall and ask the men who brought her to the meeting how to get home, indicates the stubborn determination that is part of Agnes Hancock.

However, she asked a passer-by how to get to the Shankill Road and was promptly informed, "You're on it, Mrs."

After some time a Silverstream bus did come along and she boarded it. All she could do now was to sit, and watch, and hope that she might recognise the Yates' home. As it happened she was even more fortunate than she anticipated for, all of a sudden, she spied Mrs. Yates on the street. A few minutes later they were face to face, and shortly after that, Mrs. Yates showed her the way home.

The news that Agnes could pray for people and they would be healed soon began to spread. For example, a few days after moving into her new home she was at the local shops. The lady who had been healed of the back pains was in the same shop and Agnes overheard her telling her friend what had happened. The friend had obviously some physical difficulty too and said, "Oh, I wish she'd pray for me. I'm in so much pain I don't know what to do."

Realising that a supermarket was hardly the place to be conducting such business, Agnes tried to keep out of sight, but the lady who had been healed spied her and insisted that Agnes pray, there and then, for her sick friend.

"But," Agnes protested, "I don't have any oil with me, and I can't anoint without oil."

At that the lady whipped a bottle of olive oil from off the nearest shelf, broke the seal on it and said, "Here, dip your finger in that. Nobody will mind, it's for a good cause."

The upshot was that Agnes decided to buy the oil. She did anoint the sick woman and pray for her; and she was healed. The woman immediately confessed, "This is the first time in months that I have felt no pain. How can I thank you?"

Agnes, of course, told her the Lord was the one to be thanked, and then took the opportunity to inform the assembled crowd that there was really nothing too hard for the Lord. He could do anything!

It wasn't to be very long, however, until she was to question the wisdom of those words, or at least the way she had put them.

One day she saw her friend coming across the street carrying an electric kettle. Something told Agnes that there was more to this than met the eye, so she put up a quick prayer in the form of a question. "Lord, what have I done? And what will I do? What will I say?"

When Agnes opened the door the woman's first words were, "You said there was nothing too hard for Jesus. Will you ask Him to fix my kettle?"

At that point Agnes remembered that, back in Glasgow, her own kettle had refused to work one time and her son-in-law had discovered that all it required was the plug to be pushed into the socket with a bit of extra pressure. This had reset the safety cut-out. When she tried this same remedy on the kettle now in question, there was a healthy "click" and, after pouring in a little water, the kettle worked as before.

The neighbour was delighted with this new "miracle", but Agnes realised this was the time to explain that there were some things in life that God had given men brains for. He didn't do anything for you that you could do for yourself. This was also the time to stress the importance of laying hold on eternal life. The woman listened intently and, that very day, received Jesus Christ as her saviour.

Another incident along the same lines featured a little dog. The same lady who had brought the kettle, stopped her in the street the next day and asked if she would pray for her friend's dog. Agnes had mixed feelings about this particular request, but did what she felt the Lord would have her do. Shortly after she had prayed for the dog it seemed to get a new lease of life.

There is no doubt that the Lord who made an ass to speak, and who sent ravens to feed his sevant, could also heal a little dog and thus bring joy to a human heart.

17

New Surroundings

Just as she was settling nicely into her new surroundings Agnes had a most unusual visit. Two men called at the house one day and quite bluntly told her that she would have to get out. As far as they were concerned the house that Agnes lived in should have been given to someone else, obviously someone they approved of.

The fact that she had been put there by the Housing Executive, and was the legal tenant, mattered not to them. They wanted the house, and that was it.

The Housing Executive advised Agnes to take no notice of their threats, and to tell them, if they came back, that the Executive could not provide her another house for at least a year.

After a couple of weeks had passed, and just when she was beginning to think that the incident was over, the two men returned. The message was still the same — she would have to leave — only now it was reinforced by, "You can leave the easy way, or you can leave the hard way. The choice is yours."

At the time, Agnes had no idea what they meant, but she was very soon to find out when, a few days later, a brick came through her window. It was just to be the first of many.

Some time later her daughter and family came for a few days. Agnes had hoped that during their short stay there would be no trouble. However, it was not to be.

On their very first day in Ulster a trip to Portrush was decided on. Before leaving, Agnes had prepared the evening meal so that they would have nothing to do after the long drive home but to sit down and enjoy it. As it happened, the weather wasn't the best for Portrush so they decided to return early.

When Agnes stepped through the door the sight that met her eyes was unbelievable. She stood there, riveted to the spot, surveying the scene.

The kitchenette had been broken into and everything wrecked. Human excreta had been smeared on walls, cooker, fridge, cooking utensils and crockery. What a mess! And along with it there was the horrible smell. A similar mess had been made in the bathroom. Fortunately, Agnes had had new locks fitted on the other doors and that had confined the damage.

So terrible was the damage and the mess, that her son-in-law simply threw fridge, cooker, crockery and carpets outside. At first Agnes was angry at what had been done, then hurt, that her family had to witness such cruelty and inhumanity. Yet they also saw the kind side of the local people, with neighbours coming in to offer whatever help they could.

In the midst of all this trouble she was to witness again the hand of the Lord's providence. What use is a home without somewhere to cook? And, a fridge too, is no longer looked upon as a luxury. What would she do without either? She uttered a quick prayer for help!

Some distance away, on the Shankill Road, one of her neighbours walked into Sammy Mooney's butcher shop. Sammy's mother had been an old friend of Agnes back in the Salvation Army days. When Sammy and his wife heard what had happened they despatched a new cooker and fridge, as gifts, right away. They arrived with Agnes within the hour. And they even arranged for the old appliances to be taken away.

The trouble wasn't to end there, however, for over the next number of months there was a constant campaign of harassment waged in an effort to get her out of this house. The windows were broken repeatedly, the house was burgled many times, and the men came back again, and again with more warnings and threatenings.

The whole episode culminated in the most vicious act of all, the bombing of the house, making it uninhabitable. It was obvious now that Agnes would have to leave. But where would she go?

Well, the Housing Executive are very understanding and sympathetic to such cases, and there was no difficulty in them providing alternative accommodation. The problem was that Agnes wasn't prepared to accept what they wanted to offer.

"She lives alone," maintained the Executive, "so she has no need for any more than one bedroom."

Agnes argued differently. When she had first thought of coming to Belfast she had laid a fleece before the Lord. Two bedrooms, or more, was to be the sign that God wanted her there. The harassment she had suffered; the threats, the abuse, the warnings; and now the bomb, did nothing to change that position. She would not settle for anything less than two bedrooms.

The people of the Housing Executive did everything they could to persuade her, offering several types of accommodation, but Agnes stood firm.

Two men from the church also came to her to try and persuade her that anything would be better than what she had now, and that, for her own safety, she ought to get out quick.

But Agnes was adamant and, in the heat of the moment, actually told these men exactly what the Lord was going to provide for her.

She said, "It will have at least two bedrooms, an upstairs bathroom, and I'll be able to see the hills too."

The men thought this was quite funny and, entering into the spirit of things, one of them asked, "And will the bathroom suite be coloured?"

"Oh yes," said Agnes, "it will be coloured."

The second man added, half cynically, "I suppose there'll be roses in the garden too."

When Agnes assured him that there would be, that was the end of the conversation. The two men saw that Agnes Hancock wasn't to be shifted by either foe or friend.

In the meantime she had no choice but to stay on in the house which had been bombed. That itself was an experience.

The whole back wall had been blown out, leaving both the upstairs and the downstairs open to the elements. This meant that, in reality, Agnes was confined to one front downstairs room which had to be used for living and sleeping.

Even with the house in this deplorable state there was no let up in the efforts of those who wanted her out. The final insult came just the day before she finally left the house. During the night her tormentors erected a gallows in the front garden with a rag doll hanging on it.

The legend said, "It's a rag doll this time. It'll be you next time!"

Providentially, that same day the girl from the Housing Executive called again, to tell Agnes that a suitable house had eventually been found. Would she like to come and see it?

Without hesitation Agnes asked if this was yet another one-bedroomed house, but the girl just said, "Why don't you come and have a look at it?"

Even as they left in her car the men of the fire brigade were in the back garden putting out a fire which had been lit, using Agnes' bomb damaged furniture.

When the car drew up outside the house they had come to see, Agnes thought the girl from the Executive was playing a joke on her.

But when they went inside she realised there was no joke. It had two bedrooms, an upstairs bathroom, and when she looked out of the front window, there was a beautiful view over the hills to Divis mountain. Agnes called upstairs to the workmen and asked was the bathroom suite coloured.

"Yes," came the reply, "it's green!"

And there were roses in the front garden too!

Early the following morning the removal van arrived and Agnes said a grateful good-bye. Many of the neighbours gathered round as she left and bid her their good wishes for the future.

Despite the fact that the new house was being renovated, and the clear evidence of workmen everywhere; moving into this new house seemed like heaven to Agnes.

A lot had still to be done, so when the Housing Executive workmen left at the end of the day, a friend from Millisle, Pastor Walter Gorman, brought with him another squad who worked right through the night to make the place ship-shape.

As the workmen left and the dawn broke over the nearby hills Agnes had time for a first proper look out of that front window. The words of Psalm 121 came to her and she repeated them thoughtfully:

> *"I to the hills will lift mine eyes,*
> *From whence doth come mine aid,*
> *My safety cometh from the Lord*
> *Who heaven and earth hath made"*

A great feeling of peace and calm filled her heart.

18

The Bottle of Oil

When the lady with the sore back left that Saturday morning, Agnes began to think about what she had done. Did she have the right to anoint people with oil and pray for their healing? It's true that the scriptures do say to, "Call for the elders of the church, to anoint with oil, and to pray in the name of the Lord." But Agnes wasn't an elder of any church. Or was she?

When she had been in the Salvation Army, as is the case with all officers, she had been ordained. That ordination had enabled her to conduct marriages and funerals and to perform all the duties normally performed by a minister of the gospel. The Bible says that the gifts and calling of God are without repentance. Was she not, therefore, still a minister of the gospel? She believed that she was; indeed is.

Many will not agree with her reasoning, but that doesn't bother Agnes. She believes she is acting within the will of God and suffers no qualms of conscience concerning it. The evidence of God's blessing on her ministry is proof enough for her that she is doing the will of God.

It should be added that she doesn't go around anointing with oil and praying for the sick in a haphazard or careless manner. There are many whom she never feels led to anoint or pray for. And again, she will only do the anointing herself if there isn't a man there to do it.

She claims no special gifts of healing either. Indeed, many of the people she prays for are not instantaneously cured, but are made well over a period of time. Agnes believes that God has many ways of healing. Chief amongst these is the medical profession, with all its modern scientific methods and the wisdom and compassion of its doctors and nurses.

But there is no doubt that God has given her a ministry to the sick and suffering. One or two cases of healing have already been referred to, but there are many others.

Once she was taken to the home of a man who was suffering from a serious heart condition and confined to bed. Agnes went into the room where the man was lying and both she and the man were surprised when her first words were, "You need Jesus."

The man broke down in tears and confessed, "Oh, you're so right, but I don't know how to find him." Agnes was able to point him to the Saviour and the man was immediately saved.

"Now," said Agnes, "do you believe that this same Jesus can not only save but heal you too?"

He said, "I do believe it."

Agnes anointed him and prayed for his healing. The Lord touched him, and in a few days he was up and about enjoying good health.

* * * * *

On another occasion she was asked to go to the home of a nine-month-old baby girl. She was crying when Agnes went in, and her parents told her that she had been like that almost constantly since birth.

What tension there was in that home! Before the child had been born the other members of the family had looked forward to this new arrival. Now, such was the effect of the constant crying on their nerves, that they were edgy, short tempered and impatient with each other. The child had been thoroughly examined but no reason found for her constant crying. In desperation, Agnes was sent for.

Agnes lifted the child out of the pram, saying to it, "Stop this crying until I pray for you." Then, touching her little head with oil, she prayed, "Lord, will you bring joy where there is fear; smiles where there are tears; and happiness where there is temper." When she opened her eyes and looked up, the child had a big happy smile on its face!

Agnes popped her back into the pram, gave her some toys and she began to play with them. In a few days the father was saying, "She's just a little bundle of joy and happiness."

* * * * *

Pastor Bill Dunn invited Agnes down to Banbridge for some meetings. A lady, who was due to go into hospital for a major operation, came and asked for prayer. Afterwards she felt so well that she said, "There'll be no hospital and no operation for me."

Both Agnes and Pastor Dunn felt this was unwise and advised the lady to go along to the hospital anyway. If the Lord had healed her it should stand the test of the doctors. She did go, had some X-rays taken, and was given the 'all clear'. Years later she could still say, "I have never felt better."

* * * * *

A fisherman from Portavogie was out on the Irish Sea, in his trawler, and suffered a stroke. When Agnes went to see him he lay in a coma and wasn't really expected to live. However, she anointed him and prayed for his recovery.

The man's two young sons stood by the bedside constantly, just watching, waiting and hoping for some response; some sign that their father would live. After Agnes had prayed, there was still no response and the boys looked disappointed. She turned to them and asked them each to read a verse from 1st John Ch. 5.

The first lad read from verse 14, "And this is the confidence that we have in him, that, if we ask anything according to his will, he heareth us:"

He stopped, and speaking to Agnes said, "My dad is going to be all right, isn't he?"

The second boy then took up the reading, "And if we know that he hear us, whatsoever we ask, we know that we have the petitions that we desired of him."

When he had finished he confidently cried out, "He's going to be healed!"

At that moment there was a deep groan from the sick man and his recovery began immediately. Within twenty-four hours, to the amazement of the doctors and nurses, he was discharged from hospital. Within three months he was completely back to normal.

* * * * *

Perhaps the greatest test of all to her faith in God's healing power, was when she herself was taken ill. She had been speaking at a young people's meeting where a number of those present had chicken-pox.

A few days later Agnes began to feel poorly, and when the doctor was sent for, he had to tell her that she, too, had caught chicken-pox. A couple of days after that the spots began to appear, and by the week-end Agnes felt really terrible.

On Sunday morning the telephone rang, and the caller asked Agnes how she was. Agnes began to explain how awful she felt, and what a mess her face was in with all the spots; expecting some sympathy in return. But there was none forthcoming, just a sarcastic enquiry, "What about your divine healing now?"

Agnes was taken by surprise, but even more surprised to hear herself say, "By twelve o'clock tonight someone will call, anoint me with oil, and I'll be healed." The person at the other end said cynically, "I will wait to see."

How earnestly Agnes prayed all that day for someone to come. She dared not telephone anyone, although there were many known to her who would have come, for she had said, "Someone will come."

By eleven-thirty that night she was really beginning to get worried. At ten-to-twelve she actually removed the top from her little bottle of oil. At five minutes to midnight she turned on the radio for a time check. Perhaps her clock was a little fast. But no, it was spot on time.

"Oh Lord," she prayed, "there is hardly any time left."

Just then the door-bell rang! It could have been anyone, but Agnes was certain this was the person the Lord had sent. She flung open the door and there stood Pastor Gorman and a visiting missionary.

"Come in," she beckoned quickly, "I thought you would never come. Please anoint me with oil so I will be healed before twelve midnight." She handed Pastor Gorman the oil and, just a few seconds before twelve, was prayed for.

Next morning, as she passed the mirror, she stopped to examine her face. There wasn't a spot or a mark anywhere. All the signs of the chicken-pox were gone and she felt fine.

You can imagine how much she enjoyed telephoning the cynical friend, with the good news of what God had done overnight.

*   *   *   *   *

Once the healing ministry began to blossom, Agnes found herself being invited to churches and mission halls all over the country. People want to hear her story, and to see God's power at work in the lives of the sick.

Of course, not everyone can get to a meeting. Many are housebound; some live too far away, and others live outside the country altogether. So it was suggested to Agnes that she make a tape recording of her story. A short time later, in Ballymena Elim Church, the recording was made by John Crawford. It was an instant best seller with copies going all over Ireland and many being sent overseas also.

That was nearly ten years ago and still the tape is in popular demand. Week by week the orders come in, and the tapes go out to eager listeners.

Through that one tape, several thousands of pounds have been raised to support the spread of the Gospel.

* * * * *

That brings us to the important, but often touchy subject, of finance. Many people conclude, understandably, that, since Agnes has such a busy round of meetings and, with tape sales so good, she must be 'well off'.

Nothing could be further from the truth. Those who know her well and are close to her, realise that here is someone who genuinely lives by faith.

Very often she doesn't know where the next pound will come from, except that, "The Lord will provide."

For example, in 1984, a friend asked her to accompany her to a convention in Bognor Regis, in England. Agnes knew that she didn't have the money to go, and no real prospect of getting it. When you don't have anything more than the pension coming in, there's no opportunity to save for events like this. So she would have to pray about it before giving her answer.

In due course she felt that the Lord wanted her to go, and informed her friend of her decision. The friend's husband was to make all the arrangements, booking the tickets, etc., and when it came time to pay the deposit of £26.00, he informed Agnes that he would need it in a couple of days.

Agnes hadn't told anyone of her need, being quite content to leave it with the One who had promised to provide. On the morning of the day when the deposit was required, the postman brought a letter from two friends in Scotland. A couple of nights previously they had both felt the Lord prompting them to send something to Mrs. Hancock. Their letter contained a cheque for £25.00. Agnes was able to add the other £1.00, and pay her deposit.

A few weeks later the balance of the money, £60.00, was required. That night Agnes knelt down and prayed with simple, child-like faith. "Lord, you told me to put my name down for this conference. Now I need £60.00."

Again, the night before the money was due to be paid, Agnes went to speak at a women's meeting in Richhill, Co. Armagh. At the end of the meeting she was given a lovely pot-plant. (A lot of people seem to think that she likes pot-plants. She receives dozens of them.) A cup of tea was prepared and, as they all sat around eating and chatting, one of the women interrupted.

"Mrs. Hancock, can I ask you something that is worrying me? While you were closing prayer I heard a voice — I'm sure it was the Lord — saying, 'Take up a love offering,' but I don't know how to do this."

Some of the other women overheard and, after a little discussion, a biscuit tin was passed round and an offering taken up. They wouldn't count it but just gave the lot to Agnes. When she got home she discovered there was exactly £59.00. Once again, all she had to do was to add £1.00 to what was given.

But why didn't the Lord provide the full amount? Very simply Agnes explains that the Lord was teaching her the very basic lesson that she must do something for herself.

Again and again the Lord has provided for her every need in the same remarkable way. Like the widow to whom Elijah went in the days of famine, she too, has proved that in the 20th century the same God ensures that the barrel of meal doesn't waste and the cruse of oil never runs dry.

Even Agnes' little bottle of oil was provided in the most wonderful way.

The day after the miraculous healing of the Portavogie fisherman, one of the doctors came to her house. He commented on what had taken place the previous day and expressed his belief that this was, indeed, a miracle. Then he asked if Agnes would pray for him.

He suffered from gall stones and, although everything possible had been tried to remove them, nothing had been successful. It looked as though surgery was the only answer.

When Agnes took out her oil bottle, the doctor commented on the fact that it was just a simple medicine bottle and said, "I must try and get you something better than that."

That evening he asked his wife for a little bottle she had. It was very attractive; like a miniature eastern water pot with gracious curved sides and an alabaster like sheen. However, his wife had no intention of parting with this precious ornament, and told him so.

Later, when the offending gall stones had passed through, the doctor called his wife and told her the good news.

"Well," she said, "we better let her have the little bottle then, hadn't we?"

Next morning the bottle was delivered to her door and has been in use ever since. It's one of Agnes' greatest earthly treasures.

19

Miracles!

It's strange, yet wonderful how God can turn the most difficult circumstances into something which brings Him glory.

After her house in Oldpark had been bombed, one of the first people to call was a man wearing a clerical collar. He explained that his name was Peter Timothy and that he was from the Church of Ireland. At that time he was doing chaplaincy work in the hospitals and prisons. He was sorry at what had happened to the house, and Agnes, and wanted to know if he could be of any help.

Agnes invited him in, and as they talked Peter told her of how he had come to know the Lord as his saviour, and a bit about the work he was involved in.

His visit turned out to be a real blessing, and as a result of it, Agnes became involved in the prison ministry which she still continues to this day.

She has many remarkable stories of God's power at work in the lives of those who spend their days behind prison bars.

Her very first contact with a prison family was a call to go to Daisy Hill Hospital, in Newry, Co. Down.

A young woman, the wife of a prisoner, lay dying. She

had already been given the 'last rites' of the church and was now sinking slowly into the cold hands of death. Her mother-in-law and sister sat there with her, to give what comfort they could in these last hours upon earth.

When Agnes stood at the bedside she realised that nothing could be done to help her, physically, but that there was still time to prepare her for eternity.

She explained the simple message of salvation and exhorted her to receive Christ. The young woman, who had lived in darkness all her life, didn't know how to call upon the Lord and couldn't pray without some help. But with Agnes leading her she repeated the words of the publican in Luke's gospel, "Lord, be merciful to me, a sinner."

Her sister scoffed at the idea of a simple prayer like this ensuring the salvation of a soul on the brink of eternity.

"Well," said Agnes, "let's turn to the Bible and see what it says."

The scoffer wasn't to be so easily convinced. "You'll choose something that suits your purpose," she said accusingly.

Agnes opened the Bible at Isaiah and made ready to read from chapter fifty-three. Then a new thought struck her and she acted upon it.

Turning to the dying woman's sister she said, "You give me a number and we'll make that the chapter we read from." And then, addressing the mother-in-law she said, "You choose the number of the verse."

The sister chose chapter nine; the mother-in-law, verse two. When the portion was turned up they read, "The people that walked in darkness have seen a great light: they that dwell in the land of the shadow of death, upon them hath the light shined."

What more appropriate words could anyone have chosen for someone, who at that very moment, was passing through that fearful shadow of death? So telling were the words that the one who lay dying cried out, "You see, I am saved!" In a few moments she laid her head back on the pillow and slipped out into the arms of the Saviour.

That incident soon made the rounds of the prison and was the means of opening up many doors of ministry for Agnes.

On her first visit to Crumlin Road prison, in Belfast, she was accompanied by Pauline Mooney who came along to sing. Both of them were extremely nervous for this was the first time they had ever seen the inside of a prison.

While waiting for the prisoners to assemble, the chaplain explained that Agnes would only be able to speak for about ten or fifteen minutes. Any more than that was impractical because the men got restless.

Agnes complained that she couldn't say a whole lot in that short space of time and would need longer. The chaplain wasn't convinced, but in the end they both agreed that if the men showed any sign of restlessness, Agnes would bring her message to a close.

One hundred and fifty men gathered in the prison church that day as the meeting commenced. Pauline sang two gospel songs and, as she did so, a hush descended on the place. You could have heard a pin drop! Then Agnes got up and began to tell her story. The fifteen minute deadline was soon passed and forgotten about, but the men were still listening intently. After almost an hour Agnes thought it was about time she brought the meeting to a close, and said as much. But the men protested and called out, "Tell us more, we are not going anywhere." It was an hour and twenty minutes before she finally sat down, but not before promising that they would be back another day.

What a thrill to shake hands with those men that morning; to receive their hugs; and to see their tears. What joy, too, to hear that five of them had found Jesus Christ that day.

Some months later another young man told her that, after that Sunday morning service, he went back to his prison cell and began to read the Bible seriously for the first time. Some weeks later he, too, became a Christian and, in due course, his wife and family also came to the Lord.

Today, as well as visiting those who are in prison and ministering to their spiritual and physical needs, she is not unmindful of their lack of home comforts.

That point is well illustrated by what happened one Christmas. Agnes wanted to send a gift parcel into one particular prisoner, so she asked the assistant governor if this would be possible. He asked for time to think about it, promising to let her know in due course.

When he eventually phoned he said, "How would you like to send in a parcel to all the prisoners you write to?"

This offer took Agnes rather by surprise but, never one to be overtaken by events, she accepted the challenge. It would mean finding enough supplies for almost thirty parcels.

The governor read out the list of what could be included, "Half a pound of cold meat; half a pound of cooked chicken or turkey; four apples, oranges, pears and tomatoes; one pound of loose, mixed biscuits; safety razors; sachets of hair shampoo; toilet soap; and two books."

This could prove to be a very expensive exercise, and one well beyond the means of a lady whose only source of income was the pension. She thought it would be a good idea to do some pricing, so she trotted round to the local fruit shop.

As the girl weighed the fruit, Mr. McMaster, the butcher from next door stood behind Agnes. When he heard that this was for the prison he asked, "How many parcels do you need?"

Agnes told him and he said, "Just put that down to my account." He also provided the cold meat and the turkey.

Nearby, the chemist and his staff gave the toilet soap and the razors, while Sam Mooney supplied the carrier bags nicely printed with, "Happy Christmas," on one side, and a big Santa Claus logo on the other.

Agnes used her own £10 Christmas bonus to buy the books and this was supplemented by a further gift from Sam Mooney.

What a thrill it was to drive up to the prison and hand in all those gift parcels. It must have made that Christmas a lot happier for some men.

But it's not only to those behind prison bars that Agnes ministers. She has has just the same compassion for those outside. Take, for example, the case of this next young man.

He was caught in a horrific bomb blast, and taken to hospital critically injured with, among other things, serious damage to his legs. He lay between life and death for several days while everything was done to try and save him. Eventually, the sad decision was taken that, in a desperate effort to save his life, his legs would have to be amputated.

Agnes was sent for and, at first, when she came and was told there was no hope for the lad, felt no urge to pray for any miraculous intervention, confining her prayer to one of comfort and assurance.

On the way home, however, she turned the scene over and over in her mind. Had she limited the power of God on this occasion? Was not her God, the God of miracles? Could He not raise up this young man regardless of how badly his body was broken? Yes He could!

When she stood beside his bed the second time that day, it was with a new confidence.

The young man looked up and asked, "Are you going to pray for me this time?"

Yes she was. Agnes took out her little bottle of oil, touched his head and prayed:

"Lord, touch this young man, not only healing his body, but saving these limbs, that he might be every whit whole.

In Jesus name, Amen."

Nothing dramatic happened immediately. In fact, nothing happened for twenty-four hours. His life still hung in the balance and the medical experts were more and more of the opinion that his legs would have to be removed. In fact, they decided to do just that and began to prepare him for theatre.

However, when his temperature was taken just prior to giving him the pre-med injection, it was found to be above normal. They couldn't operate! Moreover, it remained there for several days. When, at last it did return to normal, and further X-rays were taken, there was no longer any need for amputation.

From that moment he began to mend and, after further prayer, was completely healed.

Well, almost completely healed! There was just one small difficulty — when his legs had healed up, one was discovered to be about an inch shorter than the other. This meant that he had to have specially 'built up' shoes to stop him walking with a pronounced limp.

One day he met Agnes and asked her if she would pray that his legs might be the same length? Agnes thought that he should have been content enough as he was, but agreed to pray anyway.

"Lord," she began, "This is the most discontented customer we've had for a long time. Would you either put a bit on to the short leg, or take a bit off the long leg, but please, make both legs the same length."

Some time later, the young man couldn't understand why he was limping again, despite the fact that he was wearing his special shoes. He tried another pair but they were no better.

When an investigation was made it was discovered that both his legs were exactly the same length again. The unorthodox prayer had received an answer!

119

20

A *funny thing happened* . . . . .

Agnes Hancock can always see the funny side of things and, I suppose, that stands her in good stead as she meets all kinds of people. Of course, it has to be added that she does have a rather mischievous sense of humour, and can never resist the temptation to capitalize on a potentially funny situation.

Like the day she was walking up the street on the way to collect her pension.

A lady intercepted her and quite bluntly asked her, "Are you going for your pension?"

The woman was a complete stranger and Agnes felt like telling her to mind her own business, but she bit her tongue, and managed to answer civilly that she was.

Having elicited one bit of free information, the stranger enquired further. "I suppose you get supplementary pension too."

Agnes replied that she didn't.

The woman's curiosity mounted, "Do you get rent rebate."

"Yes," said Agnes, "as a matter of fact I do."

By this time Agnes had a fair inkling of what was coming next and decided to give the lady her money's worth.

"So you live alone then," continued the lady, not suspecting Agnes' answer.

"Oh no I don't," replied Agnes, quite matter of factly.

This rather took the lady aback and she asked, "How many live with you then?"

Agnes told her there were four of them altogether.

The woman was even more surprised and exclaimed, "I don't understand that one bit. Four of you — and you get rent rebate!"

Just then a voice from across the street called out, "Maggie!"

It became apparent that the woman who had been interrogating Agnes was Maggie, for she quickly excused herself and dashed off.

A few weeks later Agnes' next door neighbour mentioned that a strange man had been calling at her house several times recently.

"Who would he be," enquired Agnes.

The neighbour suggested that he was probably from the Housing Executive.

"Oh, it'll be about the repairs to the house," thought Agnes.

Next morning, at nine o'clock, the man was at the door again. When Agnes answered his call the man confirmed that he was, indeed, from the Housing Executive, and asked if he could come in.

Agnes expected him to start talking about those repairs, but when he put his first question to her she realised there was something more important on his mind.

"Are you on rent rebate?" he asked.

Agnes replied that she was.

The man said, "You live alone, don't you."

Agnes hesitated and said, "Well, no, I don't really."

The man seemed a bit impatient. "Either you do or you don't," he said.

"Well," said Agnes, already a few steps ahead, "I don't."

The man looked at her solemnly and said, "You're in real trouble!"

He opened his briefcase, took out a sheet of paper, poised his pen and asked for the name of the first person who lived with her.

Without a moment's hesitation Agnes told him: "God the Father," she said.

The man started to write, then suddenly, catching himself on, exclaimed in startled tones, "What did you say?"

Agnes calmly told him again, "God the Father."

"And what would the name of the second one be?" he continued.

"God the Son," said Agnes, still remaining quite calm.

By this time the man had begun to smile. "I'll not ask you the name of the third one, but seeing you're so smart, just tell me how much they contribute to the upkeep of the house."

Agnes was even more clever than he gave her credit for and, pointing to a text which hung on the wall, invited the man to read it.

"My God shall supply all your need," it stated.

As he left, the man jokingly suggested, "You won't be needing rent rabate any more then!"

*   *   *   *   *

One day she was asked to visit a lady in hospital. After chatting for a while she prayed for the lady and included all the other patients in her prayer. The woman in the next bed didn't really seem to be paying much attention, either to the conversation or the prayer. But when Agnes had finished she shouted over to her, "I heard you praying."

This didn't seem unusual to Agnes, so she thanked the

lady and told her how pleased she was that her ministry had been appreciated.

"But don't you understand," insisted the lady, "I heard you."

The woman whom Agnes had been asked to visit chimed in, "Do you not understand? She heard you praying!"

Agnes was beginning to wonder if she was going crazy. After all why wouldn't the woman hear her? She was lying in the next bed.

Just then the nurse passed by, and the woman whom Agnes had been asked to go and see, said to her, "This lady was praying for me," then, pointing to the woman in the next bed, added, "and she heard her."

"But that's impossible," said the nurse. "This woman's almost deaf."

At last Agnes twigged what all the fuss had been about. Once again the Lord had wrought a miracle — a miracle that hadn't even been asked for — and given Agnes the cause of many a chuckle in days to come.

* * * * *

A lot of people who ask Agnes to speak at meetings arrange transport for her. Usually it takes the form of someone calling at her house with a car, and driving her to and from the meeting.

One evening she stood watching out of the window for the car that was to come that evening. The lady who had booked her for the meeting had said that her husband would call and drive her there.

Eventually, a car drew up, and Agnes, gathering up her bits and pieces, dashed out and down the path to the waiting vehicle. Without a moment's hesitation she opened the front passenger door, stepped in and sat down beside the driver.

"You're just on time," Agnes told him.

With a puzzled look the man replied, "Am I?"

Just then another woman opened the front door of the car, looked in and said to the driver, "Who's this?"

The driver, still puzzled, answered, "I don't know."

At that moment another car pulled in behind the first one, and in a flash, Agnes realised her mistake. With a quick apology she jumped out and beat a hasty retreat to the safety of the second car. But not before making sure it was the right one.

And who says being a Christian is dull?

21

The end is not yet . . . .

As the sun lights up those familiar hills once again Agnes Hancock is already up and about.

She reads her well worn Bible and meditates on its pages. The treasures of God's word are just as fresh today as they were when she first discovered them.

Time is spent just praising God.

How wonderful it is to know the reality of sins forgiven!

How blessed to be a member of God's family!

How privileged to be in His service and to be able to minister to the needs of others.

More time is spent in supplication.

There is so much to pray for!

This needy land called Ulster!

Its people of every class and creed!

"For those who will spend all this day on a hospital bed. May they know the Lord's power."

"For those who will spend all this day behind prison bars. May they know the Lord's pardon."

"For those who will spend this day fulfilling the call of duty; whether in the army, the police or the prison service. May they know the Lord's presence."

And for herself:

> *"Teach me how to love you.*
> *Teach me how to pray.*
> *Teach me how to serve you*
> *Better, day by day."*

Her "Amen" has hardly been uttered when the telephone rings.

The conversation is brief and hurried. Someone is critically ill in hospital. Can she come right away?

The receiver is replaced, she grabs her coat, and in a few moments closes the door behind her.

Even though she has now reached the scriptural "three score years and ten," as she walks along the street to catch the bus, it's with a light step and a glad heart, for this is the beginning of another day with Jesus . . . . .

. . . . . PRAISE THE LORD!